# THE SEGMENTED SOCIETY

# THE
# *Segmented Society*

## AN INTRODUCTION TO THE
## MEANING OF AMERICA

~~~ ~~~

## ROBERT H. WIEBE

**OXFORD UNIVERSITY PRESS**
London    Oxford    New York

OXFORD UNIVERSITY PRESS
Oxford      London      Glasgow
New York      Toronto      Melbourne      Wellington
Nairobi      Dar es Salaam      Cape Town
Kuala Lumpur      Singapore      Jakarta      Hong Kong      Tokyo
Delhi      Bombay      Calcutta      Madras      Karachi

This reprint, 1979
Copyright © 1975 by Robert H. Wiebe
Library of Congress Catalogue Card Number: 74-83993
First published by Oxford University Press, New York, 1975
First issued as an Oxford University Press paperback, 1976
Printed in the United States of America

*For Douglas, Eric,*
*and Patrick*

# *Preface*

AN ABILITY TO VIEW AMERICAN SOCIETY whole, much as we might contemplate a city while circling from a plane, is worth the risks of achieving it. As long as our vision is determined solely by the place we occupy inside that society, we will almost certainly allow other people to shape our opinions and set our agendas for us. We learn early that the good life in America requires a perpetual mediation by experts. The quality of our education and jobs, the maintenance of our health and homes, the reliability of our news and advice, all depend on our success in tapping and utilizing reservoirs of specialization lying out there somewhere, and we can scarcely avoid an attitude of deference toward the indispensable experts. That posture makes us exceptionally vulnerable to their cries of alarm. When the appropriate specialist declares that the family is dying and dragging society down with it, when another announces that lawlessness is destroying America's fabric of civility, when a third warns that a constitutional emergency is jeopardizing our structure of government, we are trapped. We cannot debate the experts on their own grounds. They know so much about their subjects and we know so little. Nor can we rush about revitalizing the family and renewing respect for the law and resolving constitutional conflicts and usually much more as well. If we respond, we have difficulty knowing where to begin. Yet if we shrug and hide, we invite society to go bankrupt around us.

These pronouncements invariably arrive in bursts of urgency. Because our circumscribed lives create a multiplicity of American audiences, each sensitive to its own interests and cues, the enthusiast seeking a wide public must find a relatively simple common denominator, an appeal that will touch a generally exposed nerve. Like any product in a crowded consumers' market, a new idea must attract attention amidst a din of competitors, then stick in people's minds. Consequently, messages are sent with flares and set about with barbs. In a time of unusual upheaval and anxiety such as the late 1960s, even the normal hyperbole becomes banal and the assault grows unbearable. Each problem brings a crisis, usually a catastrophic one, and it will surely crack or shatter the culture like antique glass. Each proposal promises a breakthrough, usually a revolutionary one, and one after another they will turn the nation around like a spinning top. Why not, in one of the aptest phrases of our time, tune out?

A view of American society as a whole permits us to assess and reassemble these innumerable assertions. As we come to understand what sustains that society, what powers its operations and directs its purposes, we develop the capacity to separate what is primary from what is peripheral. Where we prize a particular value, we learn better how to defend it. Where we hate what we find, we can better calculate the enemy's strength. Following that society through history then sharpens our ability to distinguish between the lasting and the transient, and as old and new acquire more exact meanings, our estimates of possible change, when measured against America's primary traditions, rest upon a far firmer base. We even establish a more rational foundation for public policy, where we always need whatever help we can get.

The price for this sort of understanding is set by its degree of detachment. To see America as a whole places us at a distance sufficiently great to obscure much of its texture. Even a persistent adverbialness can do no more than remind us how important the subtle human interplays, the contingent circumstances, the peculiar tip to a cast of mind actually are in our everyday lives. From afar these details inevitably blur. Moreover, such an approach emphasizes social patterns at the expense of social processes. It concentrates upon relationships rather than sequences, upon the fit and function of a society's parts rather than the origins of social change and the flow of historical events. Finally, a survey of the whole subordinates a history of the themes inside American society to a history of the society incorporating them. To the statement that no one can comprehend American society without understanding American racism or imperialism, it replies that no one can understand either without comprehending the social framework that contains them. At various levels of generalization we can ask and answer different kinds of questions. The choice here derives not from a belief that one level is superior to the others, only from a conviction that the particular objectives of this essay dictate one above all others.

An overview requires its own vocabulary. Throughout the essay, the word "culture" denotes those values and habits conditioning everyday choices in such areas as family governance, work, religious belief, friendship, and casual interchange. "Society" combines these patterns with broader and more systematic realms of behavior, such as the organization of a community's life, the structure of a profession or business or religious denomination, and the formula for apportioning economic rewards. The scope of this essay is the two hundred years of American history since the Revolution, and during that span it identifies three distinctive social systems: the first lasted until the 1790s, the second prevailed between the 1830s and the 1890s, and the third has operated from the 1920s to the present. The terms "eighteenth-century society," "nineteenth-century society," and "twentieth-century society," therefore, specify qualitatively different systems, and the periods from the 1800s to the 1830s, and from the 1890s to the 1920s, mark the crucial transitions from one system to the next. These three systems are sketched in the early pages of Chapter II and explored further in Chapters III through VI. The major task of the essay, however, has been to discover elements common to all three, or in a few instances common only to those of the nineteenth and twentieth centuries. Across two hundred years of change, it has sought to define the enduring qualities of an American society.

Continuity does not imply uniformity. Diversity lies at the core of an analysis whose central argument is the persisting segmentation of American society. Segmentation, in turn, does not mean fragmentation, for the parts of American society have indeed been interlinked. What segmentation denotes is a configuration of small social units—primary circles of identity, values, associations, and goals—that have sufficient authority to dominate the terms of their most important relationships with the world outside. Some of these units have been kinship networks. Others, notably in the twentieth century, have been occupational groups, and even more in this century have been various blends of family, locality, occupation, and ethnic affiliation. The standard segments during the eighteenth and nineteenth centuries were communities, constructed around a marketing or an administrative center perhaps, or an intense religious belief, or simply a plot of land to preserve against a stream of strangers. All of these communities shared two distinguishing attributes: a membership able to visualize their social unit as a self-contained system and recognize each other's places within its scheme; and a set of indigenous institutions capable of managing the normal, everyday affairs of its members. From this assortment of small, hard pieces, ranging from a Massachusetts town in the eighteenth century to a medical association in the twentieth, Americans have built their distinctive society.

A distinctive America has still rested securely inside the

broad traditions of Western civilization. Not only has every American characteristic had its European counterpart, but very few of these characteristics have developed here in their most extreme form. Insulation has been no more severe in the villages of Vermont or Alabama than in those of Brittany or southern Italy; ethnic divisions have not exercised greater power in Chicago than in the Balkans; the cultural separation between elite whites and impoverished blacks has not exceeded the gap between patricians and peasants in Spain; social management in Washington has not been more dehumanizing than in Berlin or Moscow. The American difference arises not from a unique list of traits but from a unique pattern of relationships. American society, like any other, has been a web of tensions, an intricate arrangement of accommodations to stress and conflict that rapidly registers each sharp tug across its entire network yet resists collapse even when large portions of the web are damaged. To understand American society, therefore, we must establish its particular lines of tension, locate their special intersections, and follow its history through the outlines of this peculiarly American mesh.

R.H.W.

# Acknowledgments

My debt to the work of countless historians and analysts—a library of scholarship—is simply incalculable. This project originated during a year at the Institute for Advanced Study in Princeton, which provided an exceptional environment for pondering and exploring, and Northwestern University's generosity made that year possible. Anita and Michael Fellman dissected a draft of Chapter III; Sam Bass Warner, Jr., labored mightily to make the first three chapters comprehensible; and Neil Harris gave a full draft a sympathetic, critical reading. Sheldon Meyer patiently improved the manuscript as he eased it into print. I am very grateful for their assistance. Lonnie, my wife, encouraged me to think about American history in human terms and to write an idiosyncratic book about it in intelligible language. Douglas, Eric, and Patrick, my sons, also wanted me to finish the book, and for all kinds of good reasons it is now theirs.

*Evanston, Ill.*                                                      R.H.W.
*July 1974*

# Contents

# THE SEGMENTED SOCIETY

# ~ I ~

# On Waking from an American Dream

AMERICA'S FIRST DEMOCRATICALLY DISTRIBUTED PRIVILEGE was the right to dream, and from the first years of settlement white colonists applied it avidly and narrowly to their immediate interests. By the late eighteenth century a portion of those dreams had been converted into images of an entire society, and during the next two hundred years these national visions became integral to the meaning of America. For two centuries they consistently defined America as unique, progressive, and whole.

America's uniqueness dominated the vision of the founding fathers. A singular republican virtue, one nourished by America's customs and laws and exemplified by its revolution and industrious citizenry, distinguished this nation from all others, and out of this special merit, it was assumed, wise improvements and enlightened national purposes would regularly flow. Nineteenth-century Americans replaced uniqueness with progress at the center of their vision. In a far more dynamic version of the future, they anticipated a dramatic and infinite national climb, because America's enterprise, morals, and traditions, they declared, were perfectly suited to the laws of progress. All citizens who cared could join the endless march upward, and national unity would follow as a consequence of their common journey.

American dreams in the twentieth century, on the other hand, were preoccupied with society's cohesion. What had been no more than a by-product of republican virtue in the eighteenth century and national progress in the nineteenth now controlled the modern visions of hope. Among these, the most successful first appeared in the 1940s, flourished in the 1950s, and persisted well into the 1960s. It exalted mundane virtues. The sources of America's strength, according to this dream, lay in the practical, adaptable ways that its citizens had concentrated upon their everyday affairs as they had fanned out in packs to exploit a rich land. They had been a crowd in a hurry who squabbled, competed, swapped, then moved on, and in order to travel fast they had kept their institutions loose and their traditions light. Because they had been so eager to push onward, Americans had applied little pressure outward. Their moderation was the marvel of the Western world. While they had shoved for advantage and cursed their neighbors, they had seldom lost the ability of accepting today's compromise, for tomorrow had been their passion. With ambitions as narrow as they were intense, they could not stop to contemplate grand theories or mighty causes, and thoughtlessly they had built an elastic, open society, one that defied any neat description but somehow managed to surmount each crisis.

People who had always excelled in problem-solving, the exponents of the dream continued, learned in time to solve their problems more and more systematically. Practicality and accommodation—the American genius—were increasingly harnessed in the twentieth century to national and international purposes, as the record from the Great Depression and the Second World War demonstrated. By the 1940s, in a world suffering for its sins of ideology and hate, Americans now recognized their special talent for compromise, and with insight went power. The calamities of the past became lessons mastered: no more attempts at violent change like the Civil War, no more appeasement of dictators, no more depressions in a Keynesian economy. Self-conscious realism—a cool appraisal of the percentages and a careful use of power—underwrote the American formula of a steady, dependable progress. If other societies demanded utopia and got disaster, America would seek sensible, limited results and achieve them.

By making America's wholeness the core of its vision, the modern vision transformed the most tenuous element of previous dreams into the foundation of America's uniqueness and progress, and in the process it satisfied the pressing need for an image of national cohesion. Precisely because most Americans during most of their history had agreed upon fundamentals, they could fight and still compromise, receive newcomers from many cultures and still assimilate them into one nation, experience economic revolutions and still escape the agony of class conflict. Although extremists would inevitably appear and occasionally have their day, by definition they could only disturb, not destroy. As long as Americans retained their instinctively pragmatic ways, the absolutists of the left or right—Communists or McCarthyites—were doomed to the edges of society where they would act out their role as strident aberrations. The nation's diversity, therefore, was actually pluralism within a consensus, and the very noise of its perpetual arguments verified an acceptance of the same ground rules in a common quest for success. This democratic competition even created a kind of gravitational pull, drawing the parts into equilibrium whenever conflict threatened to exceed tolerable bounds. If one section of society grew too strong, other groups massed in a countervailing force that brought power once again into balance. In all, it was a strikingly benign vision that drew a healthy, united America from the clutter of its ceaseless, petty battles.

The method of explaining the dream was as traditional as the dream itself. For centuries Americans had defined their society not simply by European points of reference but by European frames of reference. To establish the uniqueness of America, they had relied upon negatives—the absence of something European. Thus their republicanism had been the absence of monarchy and Jacobinism, their democracy the absence of entrenched privilege, their technique of economic enterprise the absence of government direction. This had been the approach of Crèvecœur in the eighteenth century: "Here are no aristocratical families, no courts, no kings. . . . The rich and the poor are not so far removed from each other as they are in Europe." It had been the message of Goethe's oft-quoted poem, *Amerika, Du Hast Es Besser:* "America, you have it better than our old continent—no crumbling castles, no dark ruins, no useless memories and vain quarrels to trouble the soul of your vital epoch." It had made the commentaries of Alexis de Tocqueville and James Bryce in the nineteenth century so illuminating because they analyzed America so skillfully through European categories.

The dream of American consensus was conceived against a European backdrop of dictatorships and death camps, paralyzing internal divisions, and the devastations of war. What made America distinctive, it seemed obvious, was the absence of those ingrained hatreds, hard class lines, and ideological bloodbaths. The most brilliant example of this orientation was Louis Hartz's description of America as an anomaly of European history. The American nation, he argued, had been founded at a particular stage in Europe's struggle toward modernity when the contractually-minded, property-oriented bourgeoisie for whom John Locke wrote were still engaging a powerful neofeudal establishment. But America had had no such establishment. As de Tocqueville noted in the 1830s, it had been "born free"—without a feudal past, without a bastion of institutionalized privileges to smash. Naturally bourgeois, it had accepted Locke's liberalism quite literally as so many self-evident truths. In Europe the meaning of Locke had depended upon his contest with feudal authority, a dialectic whose resolution then generated a new dialectic in the continuing dynamic of European development. In America the absence of challenge had marked the end of the dynamic. There would be no French Revolution, no nineteenth-century reaction, no Karl Marx. Lacking an indigenous counterforce, America remained arrested in a liberal consensus. Like a meteor spun from the flux, America had changed only to cool and harden. "Born free," then, was the grand irony of American history, for its freedom from the European dialectic meant a perpetual bondage in liberal principles that everyone accepted because no one was capable of questioning.

While these descriptions carried undertones of criticism, the doubts came muted in a remarkably confident rhetoric. Adapting their language to their understanding of the nation's essential moderation, the spokesmen for the dream usually expressed their reservations in a reasoned, hopeful manner. Even toward opponents their mildness distinguished them sharply from the hard, hating defenders of national wholeness earlier in the century. The late 1960s shattered this decorum. Exchanges that had customarily been veiled in euphemisms now exploded in encounters. Angry people cried racism, not prejudice, mass murder, not global strategy, male chauvinist pigs, not inadvertently rude men; and their tactics required confrontations with the enemy, not discussions with the opposition. Restraints everywhere were disappearing. Obscenities once reserved for the bar and basic training became standard public idiom. In place of the antiseptic violence in yesterday's movies, audiences watched the limbs severed, the throats cut, and the brains squashed in microscopic technicolor. A passion for gambling that had sent millions to the corner bookie surfaced in many states as the government's game, and countless players followed it week by week with an intensity no other news could arouse. A lingering respect for property fell before the urge of the moment to trash and chalk and paint it. "If it feels good," read one popular bumper sticker, "DO IT!" A generation who as adolescents had listened to John and Marsha simulate the sounds of sexual intercourse on record grew up to see their counterparts perform it with variations on the screen. Sexuality and child-bearing emerged from the back room as legitimate public issues, and by the end of the decade homosexuals were demanding the same routine acceptance that any other adult preference received.

Challengers and their opponents alike met the issues of the late 1960s by drawing lines. Many used blanket categories: white or black, men or women, establishment or counterculture. A hard hat? A bigot. A long hair? A fag. Many more, in order to determine exactly who their friends and enemies were, devoted a metaphysical attention to details, to the minutiae of dress and language, patriotic ritual and racial myth. Innumerable ordinances enriched the tradition of the blue laws with long lists of prohibitions that under the guise of vagrancy, nuisance, or public health would seal each little world against outsiders. From radical cadres to rifle clubs to university administrations every group, it seemed, had its contingency plans against hypothetical attacks. The late 1960s revealed a national style that was sectarian, not pragmatic. When Americans encountered problems, they looked not for the common ground but for the boundary dividing it. Because people of all persuasions and ages and incomes adopted that style so naturally, its meaning had to lie somewhere at the heart of their society. Americans appeared automatically to know that security and comfort could only be found inside a fortress.

By the end of the decade reasonable people might wonder whether any friends lived outside that fortress. A series of massive studies, ranging in subject from Appalachia and Watts to drugs and violence, had specified the diversity, insularity, and hostility among innumerable social pockets across a national map of little domains. Those who had once lived with the happy conviction that they belonged to the manipulating ranks of society discovered that they themselves were being systematically manipulated by the elites above them. During the late sixties and early seventies, the unfolding story of America's war in Southeast Asia and the many tangled plots relating to Watergate gave these arts of puppetry their fullest documentation and aggravated doubts about the capacity of social management at any level to serve the cause of an equitable order.

Peeling a cover from American society did not significantly alter the substance underneath. The years of exposure overwhelmingly led people to conclude that their ways had been the right ways all along. Rather than revolutionizing a society, visibility ratified it, strengthening convictions and toughening resistance. The harshness, the antagonism, the deception were assimilated into a complex social system that continued to function in the mid-seventies approximately as it had a decade before, and the changes that did occur, rather than forcing a new structure, remained well within the outlines of the old.

The major casualty of the 1960s was a dream of moderation, accommodation, and cohesion, and its passing brought acute feelings of loss and betrayal. What had happened? The wages of rampant materialism, some said; or a peculiar gap between a generation reared in depression and world war and their children reared in affluence and ease; or a general gap between modern technology and a lagging standard of values. Had the rate of change accelerated beyond the human capacity to manage it? Others still hoped that the future would prove all these troubles a passing moment of confusion. Maybe the tattered cover could be mended and the old restraints restored. If people no longer looked at the ugly and talked about the sordid, they might disappear. Some tried incantation: women's liberation was merely a fad, the youth of the seventies were as conservative as those of the fifties. Many others wistfully, vaguely recalled a more peaceful past. Once rural life had been so simple; now society was impossibly complicated. Once people had run their machines; now the machines dictated to their human slaves. Once family and community had been everyone's protection; now lonely individuals stood naked before the world. Once people had found the courage to face their problems; now they searched the shelf for another pill. Or perhaps it was true, as Karen Horney and Margaret Mead had maintained years before, that a society of rootless strivers made anxiety the normal American condition. Perhaps work, money, bigness, and movement had always been the sublimations of a neurotic nation.

A more sophisticated defense against the sense of loss utilized paradox as a method of acknowledging unwelcome evidence without capitulating to it. By constructing a paradox of concentration camps for Japanese-Americans at home during a crusade to empty the concentration camps in Europe, of caste in a classless society, or of violence in a land of peace, Americans could treat their depressing qualities seriously while protecting the liberal principles they violated. Gunnar Myrdal had employed a simple version of this technique in his explanation of the color line as a unique contradiction of the American creed, and with the rising popularity of Reinhold Niebuhr's writings after the Second World War intellectuals were soon using far more complex paradoxes to interpret a wide variety of the subtleties in American society. But the broader the scope of contradictions they were expected to manage, the more strained their applications became, until paradox threatened to deteriorate into such devices as John W. Aldrich's "moral schizophrenia," a total incongruity between the values that Americans professed and the ones that they practiced.

A band of bitter critics pointed to this same spread of contradictions and called it hypocrisy. Beneath official claims to a humane world mission, an egalitarian society, and a rule of law, they found a record of imperialism, racism, and oppression, a barbarous society camouflaged with shiny rhetoric. What others had described as cooperation and accommodation they saw as cunning cooptation and bribery—the calculated uses of power—and the failure of a radical tradition simply illustrated how repressive the system had been. In effect, these rebels stood an earlier judgment of America on its head. The dream of the fifties became the nightmare of the seventies, and America emerged a monolith of madness, a consensus of the damned.

Marxism helped to discipline the indictment by specifying the social sources of America's betrayal. If a corporate class with its agents in law and politics monopolized public power, otherwise random cruelties became rational acts and official hypocrisy their appropriate ideology. Even if a dominant class was expanded to include numerous petty bourgeois allies, its ranks still limited the proportion of Americans who were responsible for their nation's crimes and opened the possibility of recruiting a mass opposition, a virtuous class to challenge the vicious. For those with the patience to wait, here were actual grounds for optimism, an alternative dream that welcomed social divisions now as the means to eventual unity and justice.

What these expressions of loss and betrayal failed to provide was a framework capable of comprehending American society. As a means of interpretation, paradox encouraged the delusion that to formulate a problem was to answer it. Filling an American chamber of horrors with hypocrisies judged an accumulation of evidence without explaining it. Like the accounts of a continually acute anxiety, reliance upon centuries of unrelieved hypocrisy required the sense of an extraordinary society that could function generation after generation at the brink of collapse, forever torn by basic contradictions in its values or forever threatened by a massive psychic breakdown. Both schemes suffered from a notable lack of historical imagination, an inability to recognize how the inconsistencies and derangements in one era might have been the normal conditions of life in another.

Marxists diminished the effectiveness of their critique by borrowing weaknesses from their primary enemy, the advocates of an American consensus. In an international context the theory of consensus had acquired its major importance as an American answer to Marxism, its Cold War antagonist, and the strongest proof of an American consensus had always been the absence of European class conflict. Domestically, Marxism won its new audience during the 1960s as a rebuttal to consensus. Just as the anti-Marxist theory of consensus had depended upon the absence of class warfare, so Marxists now verified the existence of social classes by the absence of consensus. It was a debate of intellectual gymnasts, a game of derivative categories sometimes twice-removed from their European origins and almost always at odds with their American subject. When Hartz assumed that America's simple society could not generate a dialectic of its own, he sacrificed the ability to follow an American dynamic in American rather than European terms. And when Marxists tried to force their fragments of economic dissent, ethnic factionalism, and elite privilege into a European class structure, they simply demonstrated all over again the crucial deficiencies of a European framework for interpreting an American experience.

Nothing valuable is gained by calling American society simple because it has escaped European class conflict or complex because it has produced more small centers of power and culture than any European counterpart. Since the Revolution, America has occupied a distinctive place in Western civilization, and its history has represented the contribution of an independent member, not the deviation of a dependent one. To draw upon their Western heritage, Americans have not been obliged to cross the Atlantic like tourists—as if the Roman Republic somehow belonged by a transcendent right of domain to the Papal States but not to America of the Revolution! The experiences of the late 1960s offer a striking glimpse at this special American society. It reveals itself in slogans—law and order, peace and freedom, strong leadership, government tyranny, neighborhood schools, consumer rights, black power, white power; in a simultaneous yearning for national wholeness and grasping at narrow privilege. Cruelties, suspicions, and anxieties belong at its center, and so do traditions of autonomy and egalitarianism, bargaining and accommodation. As the record of the sixties demonstrates, Americans have cultivated their differences, hatreds, and barriers. As a much longer record demonstrates, Americans have also built a remarkably resilient society capable of surviving crises with considerably greater impact than the one in the sixties. Three guidelines will help interpret this mixture of information. First, it expresses a specifically American scheme of relationships, not a negation of European experiences. Second, these elements, rather than so many curious contradictions, combine in a consistent, interdependent system. Third, this system, in order to function, has required a widespread agreement on certain fundamentals. To ignore the areas of agreement is to deny the existence of an American society, but to concentrate on them solely is to deny the history of that society.

# ～ II ～

# *The Units of Life*

A SENSE OF HISTORICAL CONTINUITY depends upon an appreciation of change. The meaning of a common American experience, therefore, must begin with the distinct societies of the eighteenth, the nineteenth, and the twentieth centuries, for each enduring quality has had to fit their very different requirements.

American society in the eighteenth century operated according to the logic of a closed system. Whatever the scope of concern—a family, a community, a new nation, an empire—the guiding assumptions in each case established a framework of rules or principles, a container of truth that defined relationships and consequences inside its bounds. Sometimes the source of these principles lay in heavenly writ, sometimes in natural law, more often in some blend of the sacred and the secular. Always, however, they existed above and prior to human actions, and therefore they always stood ready as a measure of virtue in the present and a basis for prescriptions about the future. Rarely were these truths considered incomprehensible. Although ordinary citizens might require a learned elite to explain them, their meaning nevertheless fell within the ken of human reason. Hence everyone was obligated to adapt their ways to these overarching rules, as they were commonly understood, and anyone could reasonably judge others, wherever they lived, by their degree of conformity to the same immutable principles.

Applying these principles was a delicate art that demanded quite different skills in a familiar, local setting than in a broad, impersonal one. The center of eighteenth-century society was the family in a community. Across an impressive American diversity, family and community interconnected in a great many forms, ranging from Mennonite settlements where the community almost swallowed its families to kinship systems in South Carolina and Virginia with a very loose attachment to a county seat or a region. Every variation, however, set family units to manage the particulars of everyday life in a manner that constrained each unit by the values all of them held in common. These controls, in turn, were reinforced by an assumption of the community's permanence. People expected to spend a lifetime with the same faces, the same family names, the same pattern of institutions, the same routines of work and pleasure, and as they judged these intimate relations by their superstructure of truths, they drew upon an accretion of knowledge about individuals and families and customary ways to estimate, day by day, the state of their immediate society.

The farther their vision extended beyond the community, however, the more people relied upon an explicit demonstration that the affairs concerning them in a wider environment were actually abiding by the correct principles. An obsession with the exact privileges of a colonial legislature and the precise extent of Britain's imperial power, the specifics of a state constitution and the absolute necessity of a federal one, all expressed this urge for a careful articulation as proof that the right relationship with external powers did indeed prevail. Unlike the calculations of a community's health, which gave significance to everybody's accumulated knowledge about

their neighbors and their traditions, these broad applications
of principle belonged almost exclusively to an elite. The more
a wider world affected the life of a community, the more its
members looked to an elite for mediation—to explain distant
events, to negotiate with distant authorities. During times of
crisis relationships inside a community that might otherwise
have been quite fluid tended to solidify behind a very few
leaders in order to meet an external danger. Late in the eighteenth century when Americans showed less and less willingness to deal with the outside world exclusively through elite
channels, they signaled trouble at a central point in their society's operation.

Eighteenth-century America could absorb no more than
gradual changes. When measured against immutable principles, the slightest shift in an important area automatically
sounded the alarm, not only because it threatened greater
changes to come but because it was crucial in its own right as
a disruption to an extremely sensitive network of relationships. Whether the test was a religious orthodoxy or a harmony of political powers, any deviation meant a critical im-
purity or a crippling imbalance. What appeared in retrospect
as minor differences between Old Light and New Light during the Great Awakening, as nuances in the procedure of
government following the Revolution, aroused the kind of
emotions that split communities and shattered friendships.
Would the lower and upper houses of a legislature meet in
the same building or in separate ones? Was the new chief executive His Excellency or the President? The future of republicanism might hinge on the answer.

In part, Americans could enter these debates with such passion because they understood their own character as the same
careful adjustment of components, the same minute approxi-
mations of purity, that governed their society, and character,
the most precious commodity of the eighteenth century, always deserved a fiery defense. No one thought it extraordi-

nary that James Monroe would invest about as much energy in justifying his public career as in the career itself. Microcosm or macrocosm, the imperative was stability, the security of a perfect fit between principles and practice. Consequently, when the Revolution did bring important changes to a society with no natural means of assimilating them, most of its leaders devoted themselves to resisting its radical implications, explaining its consonance with eternal truths and American traditions, then embodying that conservative judgment in the laws of the land; and voters responded by returning these same men to office. The bitter exchanges that did occur, rather than pitting demands for a grand departure against cries for reaction, almost always matched competing claims to a purer application of principles.

Abstractions that made eighteenth-century society so brittle and unyielding in some areas kept it very elastic in others. Neither time nor space shaped the minds of eighteenth-century Americans as both would for later generations. Although people obviously recognized differences between age and youth, they found little that was inevitable in the flow of life except its culmination in death. A change for the better or the worse might occur to any individual at any time; the old as well as the young studied their souls and their books in the expectation that one age was as eligible as the other to receive new insights, to improve character. Wisdom might appear in a youthful Hamilton or Madison, or in an elderly Franklin or Washington. Family, breeding, and station revealed a great deal, but the cumulative effect of the passing years told scarcely more than the moment could verify.

Eighteenth-century Americans roamed through history with a similar freedom. If civilizations, like individuals, completed a cycle of life, they also, like individuals, left a record that made sense only as immutable principles explained it. Hence Americans could cull the past for the good and the bad, the apt illustration of rules honored or violated, with a sole concern for their deductive logic from eternal truths. The Roman Republic, the Hanseatic League, the Swiss Confederation, each contained an assortment of lessons to extract and set against the verities. As late as the War of 1812, those founding fathers who still held federal office exhibited no particular embarrassment when America's declaration of war crossed in mid-Atlantic with the announcement of a major change in British policy. To Madison and Monroe it had not been a sequence of events but a violation of principles that justified the war, and any new information belonged on the scales of justice, not along a line of time.

Geography, in its usual concrete meaning, was a dependent variable in eighteenth-century America. Ties of family and belief held a prior sovereignty, and loyalties ran to the people and the ideas, wherever they were located, who served these needs. Seceding members of a church congregation either moved, carrying their community with them, or turned their backs to their neighbors, creating a community by the paths they walked. Letters united parents and children, even friends, with an immediacy that obliterated physical distance, and the deep, personal excitement that was generated by events in Europe during the French Revolution effortlessly transcended an ocean. When Americans cheered Citizen Genêt in 1793, they were greeting a brother in the cause of liberty, not a visitor from France. Place names conveyed the same orientation —the endless echoes of English towns, or the string of Republican settlements in southern Ohio that one after another memorialized Napoleon's great victories. Operating from this outlook, the founding fathers experienced no pangs of contradiction as they expanded and contracted the geographical range of their ambitions. The Federalist, who had dreamed of empire in 1799, stood behind his New England fortress in 1803 as naturally as Jefferson, who had speculated grimly on a separate nation of Virginia and North Carolina in 1799, envisaged a continental republic in 1803. Each was using geography to fulfill a purpose, not to define it.

The new society of the nineteenth century was geared to rapid change, and in order to accommodate it, Americans radically redesigned these concepts of space and time. Their world became a series of simple lines or channels along which change irrevocably flowed, and their lives a series of tests that pitted inherent worth against the hazards of change. One set of channels represented economic opportunities, and in almost all instances these followed specific, geographic lines, often related to the multiplying shoots of transportation—roads, canals, railways. Because each unit—individual or family, company or community, region or nation—perceived economic challenge as a measure of its intrinsic merit, it presumed the right to choose its own route and seek its own objectives without interference from any other unit. A properly ordered society, therefore, would comprise countless, isolated lanes where Americans, singly and in groups, dashed like rows of racers toward their goals. What happened along other tracks might be a matter of intense interest, for competitors, after all, were sprinting there, but it was seldom a matter for emulation. Each lane, testing a unique virtue, would trace a unique experience. Hundreds of communities had to learn all over again that silkworms died in America, that plank roads rotted, that imported laborers rarely revived a flagging agriculture or industry. Nineteenth-century America, as Frederick Jackson Turner observed in another context, recorded an endless recapitulation of the same experiences—a continuous demonstration of myopic pragmatism.

In a scheme of parallel endeavors, competition and monopoly were not only compatible but actually normal companions. Whatever the scope of enterprise, from a local store to a transcontinental railroad, Americans expected an exclusive realm appropriate to their ambitions where they, like their competitors in other realms, would prosper to the limits of their merit. Even when cities vied for the commerce of a common territory—Philadelphia against New York or Chicago against St. Louis—it was assumed that after no more than an interlude of uncertainty, the superior of the two would then absorb the contested area into its domain: a prolonged period of indeterminate, interlocking competition was always unnatural. Hence the primary tasks of public policy were twofold. First, it should provide sufficient space for the parallel enterprises of all its citizens, a requirement of such vast proportions that it made nineteenth-century America a study in insatiable land hunger. Second, public policy should guarantee freedom within each lane. A legal system to delineate the boundaries between parallel enterprises, and the passionate differences this system generated, defined the most critical public issues of the century. During these angry debates, charges of "monopoly" were directed not at exclusive privilege itself but at the intrusion of someone else's privilege into a sphere that the accusers considered their own.

A second set of lines marked the life span of individuals. As a corollary to their economic ambition, Americans assumed that they would normally move in search of better opportunities and that their initial departure would probably occur as soon as they became adults. Lives were now charted in sequences of time, with childhood as the crucial period of preparation, young adulthood as the most severe period of testing, and the later years as the increasingly predictable consequence of what had accumulated over a previous lifetime. To ready them for the unknown, children were taught a few, simple truths as their inviolable guides in life, and young adults were then scrutinized to see how thoroughly they had internalized these absolutes and how effectively they could operate from them. The models of success were invariably people of full maturity who could display a long record of strength against temptations and vacillations; the youthful patrician had disappeared from the gallery of American leaders. Although middle age brought a degree of security, nothing fully released individuals from the imperative to prove themselves, to verify that their lines were indeed ascending ones. Life's path was determined by a ceaseless flow of cause and effect, and at any time the force of a bad decision might wreck the work of many decades. Who knew the flaws hiding in even the finest careers? For individuals as for all units of enterprise in the nineteenth century, the commandment was grow or die. Any pause risked decline in a world of sudden challenges and shifting opportunities, and males in particular were driven on a lifelong quest for improvement that would repeatedly validate their personal worth.

What might have seemed the atomization of American society was in fact an age of unusual community strength. It was an internalized community that individuals carried with them, and it was a replica of this community which they sought as a place to settle. Rootlessness, as distinct from mobility, implied the absence of both a moral base and an adequate setting for economic enterprise. The community, like so much else in nineteenth-century America, acquired a new geographical exactness to meet the responsibilities it was now expected to manage. Inside its boundaries lay a preserve where members prepared themselves to meet the challenges of a wider world. There they amassed their moral and economic resources for a successful outward thrust, and they guarded their community against any influence that might damage their peculiar values and rights, their special moral stamina and special cluster of ambitions. Because strange people constituted an omnipresent threat to the community in an era of mobility, members devoted particular attention to the sifting of newcomers. In this task, as well as in interpreting the good and the bad tendencies of a broader society, they came to rely upon shorthand devices that sorted people by their surface characteristics: their skin color, their demeanor, their public habits. These very surface qualities, in fact, were the ones they emphasized in the rearing of their children. In a society of small, absolutistic domains and compelling material ambitions, it was perfectly consistent to resist cultural novelty with the same sort of intensity that they invested in economic or technological innovations.

Institutions extending beyond the community operated by the same formula of a few absolutes thoroughly internalized, infinitely applicable. Political parties and religious denominations, the public school movement and civil service reform, a legal profession and a fraternal organization, all relied upon a small set of principles and procedures—a kernel of truths— that could enable people widely dispersed and scarcely in communication to pursue their activities with a firm sense of common purpose. A carefully marked Bible or Blackstone, Theodore Weld on slavery or Horace Mann on education held the essentials, and an unwavering dedication to the simple truth completed the links of an effective, if almost invisible institution. In its broadest application, this logic explained the course of the entire society. The nation, like any other unit, was following its own irresistible sequence of cause and effect, and it also was bound by the truths at its core. Because anything that violated its absolutes—the wrong tariff law, one slave, an evil President, or whatever seemed critical from the perspective of a particular community— threatened to bring disastrous results, Americans remained constantly alert for that first, perhaps half-hidden sign of a momentous turn. A change at the core of society would affect the whole pattern of tracks inside it, ultimately altering the destinies of individual, community, and nation together.

The Civil War demonstrated the operations of this social system without significantly damaging it. The Missouri Compromise, banning slavery above 36′ 30° and allowing it below, had established channels of parallel growth for the North and the South that eventually merged in the trans-Mississippi territories. By the 1850s the natural urge to comprehend a complex course of events by a crucial absolute—a central cause— had elevated slavery and free soil to the level of explanatory truths about the South and the North, and the imperative to grow or die now applied to the triumph of a section's truth in the territories. Either one or the other would have to prevail; the issue could not linger. In a world of inevitable expansion or contraction, people in both the North and the South increasingly interpreted the pieces of evidence about them as a sequence of cause and effect that would extend either slavery or free soil throughout the nation. To more and more southern leaders, the evidence told them that their grand vistas of space and opportunity were rapidly closing, a prospect that Daniel Webster among others had already pictured for them, and they made a dramatic shift at the core—secession—in order to break the deadly flow of events, preserve their special sources of moral and economic strength, and demarcate their own safe paths for development. In the North, secession violated fundamental law and conjured visions of an expansive evil permanently at hand. By a comparable logic from central absolutes to inevitable consequences, the decision for war followed.

The mark of war branded millions of lives. Slavery was abolished. With major changes in the southern economy came a new centrality for its towns and small cities. A general process of industrialization was greatly facilitated. Yet contemporaries overwhelmingly interpreted the war as abnormal, and the lessons they drew from it were largely negative and heavily conservative. The willingness of so many southerners to read the war as a judgment of failure and seek new leaders for a new departure, the willingness of so many northerners to accept adjustments in the law as proof of a redeemed society, and the eagerness of people everywhere to return to their economic channels indicated how well the fundamentals of nineteenth-century society had survived the war. It would require several decades more to undermine the economics of parallel development and force Americans to reconsider this open, expansive system of geographical lines.

In the twentieth century these parallel tracks were redesigned to form the interlocking pieces of a puzzle. According to a pattern that was organized around productive and distributive business, the units of the new society acquired their definition from the functions that they performed in a single, national system. A logic of relationships within this system replaced a nineteenth-century logic of countless scattered enterprises, each of which American society had been expected to honor and accommodate. Just as citizens had once contested boundaries across space, they now competed along the borders of occupational privilege, and the antagonists were determined by business specialties, agricultural products, professions, and labor skills rather than by communities, states, regions, and the economic ambitions that these units of nineteenth-century society had supported. In the twentieth century, what one did superseded where one did it as the initial, controlling question.

A system based on social functions splintered the elements of wholeness that had characterized nineteenth-century America. Instead of assuming an essential sameness at every level of society—individual, family, community, nation—each functional unit accentuated its own particular qualities that related to its role in the system, and the system itself was then presumed to operate by still another set of rules. Rather than acknowledging the presence of general absolutes, each subdivision claimed a separate truth, one accessible only to insiders with a unique training and experience. A multitude of functions, a multitude of specializations, yet each person could master very few, probably only one. In order to succeed, individuals had to concentrate on a single specialty; in order to survive, they had to rely upon an array of specialists in those many critical areas beyond their knowledge. What originated as a way of organizing work and responsibilities in an urban-industrial world thus spread into a pattern of life. Without expert guidance, who could prepare a balanced meal, evaluate candidates for the local judiciary, understand

one's children, relieve headaches, enjoy sex? An endless parceling of expertise transformed individuals themselves into
an agglomeration of functions—wife or husband, mother or
father, consumer or citizen, hostess or handyman—each offered as a solemn, sovereign obligation and none necessarily
integrated with the others outside the individual's schedule of
daily activities.

New national elites inspired and dominated this society. It
was the requirements of their work, the pursuit of their objectives, that created a system of functions transcending the
older geographical attachments, and it was they who monopolized its primary benefits. Although Americans could never
agree on one scale of importance to rate the members of the
modern system, the usual measures—significance in economic
production and distribution, degree of specialization, amount
of wealth—promised little recompense for the majority with
routine or menial jobs. In the nineteenth century a society of
innumerable little communities had multiplied local winners, held the distance between the top and the bottom of a
community to manageably human proportions, and protected
the self-respect of many citizens with small incomes but good
reputations. A single national standard, on the other hand,
funnelled a few winners to the top, dramatically extended the
distance from there to the bottom, and stripped an anonymous poor of their residual sources for respect. Millions of
Americans resisted these consequences. As supplements or re-
placements for this encompassing national scale, a wide variety of people—local elites, ordinary citizens in the countryside
and the cities, and the impoverished everywhere—turned instead to some version of the old-fashioned cultural norms, personal networks, and attachments to place as their defense
against the national system's demeaning evaluation of their
lives. Although no one could ignore the omnipresent values
of the new elites, the casualties of the modern system could
modify or even defy its judgments, and as a result they devel-

oped subtle shadings of qualitative difference throughout a
society that was now divided not by many applications of a
single social formula, as in the nineteenth century, but by
many social formulas with contradictory elements: education
versus ethnicity, impersonal skills versus personal connections, economic function versus place of residence, in complex variations and combinations.

What mitigated the effect of these new social divisions was
a common commitment among almost all Americans to the
rewards that the national system generated. Whether their
source was a corporation or a distributor of credit, a law or
an administrative agency, a direct government payment or an
indirect government subsidy, an overwhelming majority depended upon the modern scheme of economic functions for
their well-being. Even those who rejected its values fought
grimly for their place in a structure that determined their
livelihood, and such an intense involvement gave a deep, national toughness to the system. A common commitment to the
goods and services that this system so grandly displayed served
as an equally powerful source of social cohesion. Indeed, less
successful participants in the system, as compensation for
their meager satisfactions from work, proved to be especially
ardent consumers. The cardinal test of the system, therefore,
became its capacity to guarantee each constituent group a regular flow of rewards, a predictable payoff, and weak and
strong alike combined to defend it against any radicals who
might jeopardize these crucial procedures of distribution.

A society of interrelated parts required leaders with a refined talent for management. To motivate those who end-
lessly repeated a single routine and to regulate a multitude of
groups in the service of economic productivity and social
peace would have taxed any leadership. Yet this system was
also dedicated to change. Because it was predicated on a con-
tinual economic growth, it welcomed new products, services,
and technologies, and it accepted the arrival of new func-

tional groups whenever these seemed necessary either to increasing productivity or to maintaining peace. Imaginative responses to flux placed the highest valuation on leaders who could maneuver with the forces around them—adapting here, pressuring there, always remaining alert to the use of one group's ambitions for another group's goals. Premier leadership was sensitive manipulation, the deft guidance of diverse people by means and toward ends that they would never recognize. As these skills came also to cover a complex pattern of international involvements, the touch of the invisible hand required even more delicacy. Like all members of the system, its leaders received their rewards for results, not for the procedures producing them. Their particular specialty was the technique of management, and their public policies were judged by the only standards inherent in the system: the social functions they performed.

Five fundamental conditions of American life combined to form a base beneath these very different societies, a foundation that not only set the broad outlines for each century but also sustained certain essential qualities from one to the next. One of these conditions was an expanse of land—the initial impression of explorers and settlers, the invitation to dreams of empire, the grand vision of Turner's frontier society. Although the changing relationships between stretches of space, on the one hand, and transportation, communication, and social integration, on the other, significantly altered the meaning of land over the centuries, it nevertheless remained at the center of American aspirations for three hundred years after the establishment of Jamestown. During the seventeenth and eighteenth centuries people tried to contain its benefits within a fixed scheme of life. They moved no farther than necessary to find the land, and their purposes for acquiring and using it drew even the most successful back home to found great families and stand atop their communities. Only in the nineteenth century did a beckoning space give America its strong outward thrust. While people in the nineteenth century still sought land above all to farm, they also employed it increasingly as a means or a medium: a source of credit and speculation or a route for trade. Both in the countryside and in the city more and more Americans were devising ways to broaden their domains, link isolated centers, tap and transport raw materials. By the nineteenth century their sense of opportunities had come to rely so heavily upon matters of where and how far that to call America future-oriented was to say, once again, that it was space-oriented.

Beginning in the early seventeenth century, an expanse of land pulled against preconceptions of good order. Where would virtue reside in raw, distant places? Puritan fathers lamenting the spread of the faithful, seaboard patricians disdaining the styles and needs of backcountry colonists, British policymakers drawing a line in 1763 to dam the spill of settlers, New England Federalists despairing the loss of liberty through the Louisiana Purchase, southern Republicans bemoaning the triumph of barbarism across the Appalachians, and eastern centers resisting a war for western expansion touched only a few peaks of an uneven but persisting concern about the dangers of sprawl. Americans had reason to worry. Until about the middle of the nineteenth century the spread of people steadily outdistanced the means of transportation and communication to connect them. Even as the balance began to tip toward national integration with the frantic construction of roads, canals, then railroads, telegraph, and telephone, these strands still disrupted old relationships as they were organizing new ones. For each town that thrived, many others rotted or died. Cities attached to a canal or railroad were often wrenched from an existing network of local or regional interdependence and drawn into a new scheme of trade and finance, news and culture. Because these intrusions of progress came so rapidly in a century of industrialization, a tradition of mutuality, of customary relationships, could offer little resistance. In the nineteenth century the ties between a city, even a town, and its surrounding area almost always changed by the rules of economic advantage, not by the varying elements of custom and profit that prevailed in many parts of Europe.

Open land was a vacuum as well as a magnet. From the earliest days of settlement it invited those people who had differences to solve their problems by separation instead of accommodation. Rather than adjust, they parted. Where the sectarian spirit already ran high, as in Puritan New England, a fragmenting process began as soon as the settlers landed and continued to sow clumps of people apart from each other—to drive off dissenters, to start the trek for another river valley, another seaport, another free place. Where hostile Catholics and Protestants found themselves neighbors, as in Maryland, they fought only as long as it took their camps to disperse. Everywhere it accentuated a tendency to preserve particular beliefs, to prize homogeneity, to leave all antagonists holding some position triumphant. Differences were spread across space rather than managed within it.

The tensions over deep cultural divisions, therefore, were pushed outward where distance lessened the likelihood of people reconsidering their hatreds or, in most cases, of acting upon them. Inside the communities life concentrated increasingly upon distinctions among the likeminded, giving daily human relations a peculiar, prickly quality of nuance. As a consequence, local leaders came early to have a special role. Rather than assisting diverse groups to function within a common sphere, they articulated those values everyone was expected to accept. They became experts in doctrinal exactness—not theorists who drew a higher synthesis from a clash of beliefs but refining sectarians who found new phrases to give old truths a greater precision and to sharpen the lines distinguishing purity from contamination. When they met in larger assemblies, they brought both the talent and the charge to maintain their community's truth. Thus leadership at this level required the skills of division and apportionment, a granting of rewards so that they translated the effects of space and separation into solutions of apartness and inviolability. Whether the participants were New England towns, Pennsylvania factions, or Virginia families, compromise meant parceling, and parceling rested on a begrudging toleration of each group's right to retain its own ways. By the mid-eighteenth century, colonial leaders had become masters of such arrangements. It would prove a powerful heritage, one by which Americans, so puzzlingly brittle and contentious to the British, transferred a colonial tradition of politics and social harmony into their new national life.

A second fundamental condition of American life, cultural diversity, accentuated these qualities of particularism. From the seventeenth through the nineteenth century, a land of immigrants and insular compartments placed an exceptionally high premium on an acute awareness of cultural differences. Early in the colonial years this outlook was one natural expression of Reformation principles: that belief and authority were indivisible; that society, therefore, required an identity of civil and religious purposes; and that the symbols of both must be immediate and personal. In their American version, however, these principles applied to units of notably small scope. What in Europe was presumed to cover provinces or nations operated in America to separate communities. Broader systems—the attempts to impose Anglicanism in the southern colonies, for example, or seventeenth-century schemes for "association" among New England congregations —faltered before a jealous localism. By the middle of the eighteenth century the waves of pietistic enthusiasm and doctrinal re-examination called the Great Awakening, which some ministers at first saw as the source of a new moral cohesion, had shattered the remnants of cultural unity throughout the colonies. By exposing and then formalizing innumerable religious differences, the Great Awakening heightened the importance of local self-determination and forced public policy to honor the cultural autonomy of these many new units. Although vestiges of an established religion lingered for several decades, a full range of cultural issues now belonged to a realm of political barter. On all but the local level, the dream of that sturdy dissenter, Roger Williams, had been realized: religious and civil authority were separated. But the result—in fact, the purpose—of that victory was to weld this authority inside each community and protect it against any higher power. Within these segments, principles reminiscent of the Reformation endured.

The expansive, entrepreneurial world of the early nineteenth century brought a new range of threats to the community's cultural integrity. To keep its territory pure by the old standards of a stable sectarianism was no longer possible in a highly mobile society, nor could members of these larger, fluctuating communities maintain the same sense of human continuity, of personal qualities unwinding over the years. Consequently, they came to rely less and less on the details of belief. Religious denominations that would never have tolerated cooperation with each other in the eighteenth century selectively, uneasily submerged enough differences in many communities to form Protestant fronts. But as the rules of private belief loosened, the rules of public behavior tightened. What was no longer available through intimacy revealed itself through standardized tests of the external record, uniformly applicable criteria that could sort virtue from vice among people they barely knew. Although these tests varied considerably among communities, they shared a common emphasis on readily observable characteristics that lent themselves to quick, clear judgments. Public behavior, once merely signifying the state of the soul, had itself become the substance of virtue.

The most important tests of the nineteenth century measured acceptability by appearance—skin color, dress, deport-
ment—and by customs—language, family governance, religious
ritual—according to broad racial and nationality stereotypes.
Where judgments by appearance had been used in the eighteenth century—among a cosmopolitan, seaboard elite, for instance—the standards had been strikingly different: LaFayette
and von Steuben, Albert Gallatin and Stephen Girard, had
not been sifted through an ethnic screen. Even traditional enemies now acquired new meanings. For many Protestants,
"Catholic" became indistinguishable from "Irish," and its
evil, rather than the strict terrors of eternal damnation, related more and more to the horrors of earthly behavior—corruption, licentiousness, alien dictation. Waves of immigrants
promptly learned to apply these rules both in their own behalf and to each other. Whatever their original inclinations
had been, they gathered into self-conscious ethnic clusters as
their basic defense in a society that was already ordered by
such categories. Yet neither old families nor new arrivals
could depend upon maintaining their exact choice of ethnic
standards. Vague and often unstable mixes of white Protestantism were the lot of most nineteenth-century communities,
and many immigrants relinquished their natural identification with a European province or town in favor of nationality
groups because America could offer them nothing better.

The effects were a gross but powerful technique of definition and division. The deep etching of a color line, the
proliferation of nationality stereotypes, and the ethnic sensitivity of politics, education, and a host of voluntary associations attested to its primacy in the nineteenth century.
Even in the exceptionally fluid world of the cities, urban
dwellers did their best to approximate the ideal of ethnic self-
determination because it had become their fundamental
American right. Where weak, scattered people could not protect themselves from an outside cultural domination, they did

indeed belong at the bottom of society. Hence their first collective action usually demanded this essential privilege, and these assertions, in turn, helped to give local politics its crucial, emotionally charged place in nineteenth-century society. The efforts of most white Americans brought substantial returns. Attempts to control other people's cultural lives through prohibition or Sunday laws or an unacceptable model of public education generally lacked the stamina to overcome the fierce resistance they encountered. The most noteworthy aspect of nineteenth-century nativism, aside from its virulence, was its extremely thin record of accomplishments. Even as space was losing its power to insulate the parts of society late in the century, ethnic consciousness, its traditional American ally, continued to maintain the walls with an impressive resourcefulness.

A third fundamental condition, military security, also operated most effectively in the nineteenth century, although its influence, too, extended throughout American history. From a remarkable sequence of circumstances, as C. Vann Woodward and others have noted, America enjoyed a unique freedom from both immediate military threats and the experiences of war. Although Indian resistance to white colonization produced a number of bloody conflicts, these tended to be brief and localized, and after the mid-seventeenth century they actually touched a fast-diminishing proportion of the colonists. Of course the weak coastal settlements of the seventeenth century were extremely vulnerable to European warships, and well into the eighteenth century the British navy continued to spread an indispensable cover over the colonies. Aside from that protection, however, America's location meant that any European nation would have to make an inordinate investment in order to devastate rather than sporadically damage the colonies. The Atlantic to the east, the rugged terrain to the north and west, and the decline of Spanish power to the south buffered America from all except the most dedicated military efforts, even in an age of war and conquest. Who could calculate the enormous significance of surviving its own revolution and the generation of warfare that followed it with only minor military occupations and scattered domestic destruction? By the nineteenth century the possibility of a crushing defeat from abroad had disappeared, and by the early twentieth the United States held the option of entering or avoiding European battles as it chose. Not until the advent of rocketry and nuclear weapons did it face a serious prospect of overwhelming military disaster. Even then, only faded southern memories of the Civil War gave Americans any consciousness of war's searing effects at home. Throughout its history, in other words, America had escaped a fundamental part of life almost everywhere else around the globe.

Security relaxed the social fabric. Simply and profoundly, freedom from military imperatives meant freedom to go about one's affairs. In Europe these demands compelled at least some consolidation and common purposes; in America they could rouse little more by the nineteenth century than a feeling that military emergencies would somehow be met as they arose—if in the meantime destiny's hand had not interceded. Major portions of Europe emerged from the era of the French Revolution with a new awareness of the nation as a social whole that bound even those who hated or despised each other to an ultimate accommodation. Because Americans escaped the traumas of war, they also escaped that sense. By an American logic, if people hated or despised each other, they could simply live apart. An ultimate accommodation was not merely unnecessary; it was unnatural. Assuming the sovereignty of their communities, Americans could follow the dictates of their everyday values with less interference than the people of any comparable Western society.

Only extraordinary dangers could have tied Americans to the needs of military readiness, for as Louis Hartz has outlined a fourth fundamental condition, America was "born free" of an extensive institutional framework. Colonial America evolved without the social skeleton that a monarchy, an aristocracy, an established church, and their supporting and administering retinues might have provided. The extension of these agencies from Britain seldom contributed more than an occasional presence, a limited locus of power, and a broad norm; they did not offer effective organizing devices for colonial society. Although the last feudal policies had disappeared in England during the seventeenth century and aristocracies throughout Europe had become purchasable and fluid by the mid-eighteenth, an institutional superstructure remained to define maneuvers and ambitions, relationships and revolutions. For the purposes of illuminating an American difference, the malleability of that superstructure was far less significant than its presence as a rough webbing for social change. While European dissenters in the eighteenth century developed ideas in response to these institutions, the founding fathers relied to a considerable degree on ideas about those ideas.

"Born free" in America meant born in pieces. So little resisted the pulls of a local attachment. Michael Kammen and Paul Lucas have indicated how deep the rooting in local affairs and how suspect the involvement in a larger establishment had already become by the late seventeenth century. "Effective authority in the eighteenth century was local authority," Michael Zuckerman has written of Massachusetts, "and a governor had to accede to it if he wished to govern effectively"—an assessment that applied equally well to a wide variety of American settings. In both crown and proprietary colonies, power normally flowed not only from England to the governor, who was dependent upon the provincial interests encircling his capital, but from there into the interior where administration either adapted to local conditions or generally failed. Declarations from England were heard as faint echoes in an inland center, and their ritual quality during much of the eighteenth century expressed their irrelevance to the usual functionings of colonial life. Although the periodic suppression of uprisings established boundaries to dissent, that did not appreciably affect the sources of daily authority.

Cries of outrage changed nothing. Puritans who bewailed a lost cohesion, colonial officials who begged for reinforcements against an eroding authority, and British theorists who recommended the imposition of a stabilizing aristocracy loosely described a state of society without altering it. The few attempts to implement a centralized policy met hard responses, and persistent threats of a detailed rule from London eventually moved the colonies to revolution. A generation later, the Federalists lost national power when they experimented with a comparable policy. Where traditions of direct, local representation dated in some instances to the early seventeenth century, Americans rejected virtual representation through either the British Parliament or a Hamiltonian elite for what it was: a means of centralization. Following Jefferson's inauguration in 1801, the Republican commitment to a detached, benign surveillance sufficiently divested the national government of any pretensions to rule that after 1807 it frustrated the Jeffersonians themselves when they also sought to mobilize America. Each defeat stripped a layer of integrators from American society. The failure of imperial politics, then High Federalism, and finally the remnants of an eighteenth-century patrician leadership, one by one, left in their wake a triumphant particularism. Between the 1760s and the 1810s, the unnatural discipline of a central command not only slackened whenever the press of crisis eased, but it ceased altogether as soon as the European wars ended. It would be difficult to argue that America responded better in the 1820s to direction from Washington than it had in the 1750s to rule from London.

Throughout the nineteenth century America remained a

society without an institutional core. Except for a brief period in the 1860s, Washington served largely as a clearing house for a quite limited range of problems. The narrowness of federal responsibility that struck Alexis de Tocqueville and Michel Chevalier in the 1830s was still there late in the century to impress James Bryce: "Political light and heat do not radiate out from the centre as in England. They are diffused all through the atmosphere. . . ." As de Tocqueville recognized, the issue transcended politics: "America has no great capital city, whose direct or indirect influence is felt over the whole extent of the country. . . ." No London or Paris, even Madrid or Rome, served as a source of national standards and information, a place where elites mingled and merged, a focus for awe and envy and anger. Republicans had established Washington specifically to avoid that kind of concentration, and by the time New York City had accumulated some of these cultural powers, a sturdy tradition of plural centers, an assumption of many norms exemplified in many places, restrained its importance at least as much as its separation from the nation's political capital. Appropriately, no great newspaper or magazine—or even a handful of these—enjoyed national dominance. From the mid-eighteenth century, when coastal elites were mimicking British ways, through the early twentieth century, when reformers were exchanging views on German civic practices, European models exercised a greater influence over American cultural and social standards than did those of any domestic city.

Institutions grew locally to serve localities. In politics or law enforcement, religion or education, the connections from community to community in the nineteenth century were always kept compatible with those primary attachments. Founding a voluntary association in response to each new issue also suited a society lacking institutions of general competence. Every reform had its own agency, every urban problem its own committee of notables. As nineteenth-century Americans looked beyond their community, they tended to invest their loyalties in small, prudent bundles, and they required a great many vehicles to carry these parcels into a wider world.

Inside the community, such habits helped to preserve a tight local integration. Spread across an entire society, however, they created a remarkable institutional looseness. Without centers of scientific information, Americans went abroad to learn critical skills and borrow major innovations. Without a framework of working-class culture, laborers adapted to their communities or scattered among their neighborhoods. Without national patterns of deference, the most successful either abided by local customs or when the opportunity allowed, retired within social compartments of their own. After a period of tentative interaction among the revolutionary generation of patricians, nationwide communication among America's elites lost a common idiom, an accepted means of identification and discourse that would have enabled one group of local leaders to recognize and cooperate easily with another. When industrialization struck with full force late in the nineteenth century, no alternative scale of national values mediated its arrival. With a peculiarly American intensity, industrialists followed the logic of their company's development, neither tempered nor hampered by an established standard of national obligation, a sense of general social responsibility. Institutions that had grown far past their origins simply pushed as far as they could go. No ceiling, no challenge at large in the nation, restrained them.

Economic abundance, which David Potter so sensitively explored, was a fifth fundamental condition of American life, one that caught the eye of almost every foreign observer and the imagination of almost every American. Its influence derived from the exceptional diversity of its sources. Unlike Arabian oil, for example, American abundance neither drew society's energies to a single center nor lent itself to a simple monopoly. Unlike the commercial-industrial concentrations of England or Japan, it did not even direct activities into a particular category of pursuits. If at any one time some area brought appreciably greater wealth than others, these points of attraction not only shifted quite radically, sometimes decade by decade, but were always surrounded by a broad range of alternatives that promised their own substantial returns. An overview of America was a panorama of economic choices —farming the land and utilizing its forests, commerce at home and abroad, mining and manufacturing and finance, and the countless subdivisions and subsidiaries of each.

In no sense was the result equal opportunity. Special advantages from wealth and prestige and favoritism varied as greatly as the economic options themselves, and the inclination to monopolize particular privileges added to a labyrinth of hardship and exclusion determining the actual exercise of these choices. What abundance produced instead was a general dispersal. First, it diffused power. Many centers of economic activity so complicated the process of domimating a broad domain that even ambitious people tended to make the most of their own bailiwicks. Any grand expansion simply required too intricate a pattern of alliances and faced too varied an array of opponents. Moreover, as new opportunities contined to open, they repeatedly shifted the base of wealth and prestige. Although the reshuffling of economic elites was seldom rapid or chaotic, it was steady enough to limit accumulations of power and confuse the tactics of competition.

American abundance also diffused attention. The many points of attraction, each with an impressive promise, each with its own peculiarities, subdivided society into innumerable interests that took their differences for granted and found their common concerns only under duress. In its normal state America was a scattering of visions and energies, a society of mutual preoccupations where even sustained dialogues were rare. Finally, abundance diffused economic rewards—not equitably but widely. In part, this dispersal was a corollary to the great range of profitable opportunities. Above all, an almost chronic scarcity of available, appropriate labor in an economy of endless technical adjustments forced a flow of benefits downward, a distribution that at the lower levels astonished rich visitors and impoverished immigrants alike. The effects of this shortage were always complex; it underwrote black slavery as well as white mobility. Nevertheless, by raising most Americans well above a level of starvation, it gave "basic" a distinctive meaning in the issues that would dominate their society.

With opportunity rather than survival determining their goals, Americans could act on the assumption that only God and nature, not a crowd of competitors, set the odds on their ventures. In an abundant economy communities could isolate themselves without necessarily paying the price of a subsistence living. Particularly in the nineteenth century, as Americans spread across the continent, the compatibility of growth and separation received regular, reinforcing demonstration. Because groups were not inevitably snatching for the pieces of a fixed total, their success or failure seemed to bear no relation to the interactions of a larger society, nor did their struggles for advantage require one group's destruction in order to certify another's victory. No contest was inherently a single, last chance. Even the suspicion of outsiders did not automatically involve the fear that they would steal from a limited store of community gains. Such a broad arena for competition softened its effects and encouraged Americans to believe that its most natural operation was row upon row of private, walled paths.

In time, abundance threatened to undermine the society it had helped to establish. Dreams of bounty impelled people to cover the nation's best land and pack its cities, master its distances and industrialize its economy at a startling rate of acceleration, and by the end of the nineteenth century, the Jeffersonian vision of a gradually unfolding paradise of farms and villages had been transformed into a sense of filled space where geography could no longer ensure either wealth or separation. It was at this juncture that abundance most critically and explicitly preserved America's traditional ways. The heart of the modern system of functions was a pattern of payoffs that rewarded strong groups with spheres of general autonomy and promises of enlarging wealth. Because these rewards were so impressive, more and more Americans shaped their aspirations to fit the occupational system, to demand that they, too, receive a guaranteed sphere of their own. Only in a land of plenty with its presumption of an ever-expanding economy could people have sustained their faith that interdependent groups living side by side need not break the barriers between them and scramble over an apportionment of the nation's wealth. While abundance had been facilitating separation since the seventeenth century, in the twentieth it rationalized an entire system, a compact society of interrelated but insular parts.

The centrality of abundance in creating a society of small, self-consciously distinct units made it equally important as a rare source of common vocabulary, a means of communicating the essence of their lives across the innumerable gaps that divided them. Among themselves Americans employed a language of how much, how many, how far to express subtle blends of amount and quality, and they assumed some capacity on the part of their audience to translate these statements into an assessment of character and piety, skill and resourcefulness, to recognize them as simultaneously the by-products and end-products of certain virtues. Because Americans learned early to reach each other through a quantitative idiom, they expected Europeans also to comprehend the quality of their society in terms of the size of farms and the extent of forests and the number of people and the statistics of production. When Europeans insisted upon taking these claims as no more than crude boasts, Americans properly felt misunderstood. But neither resentment nor repetition could impose an American construction on words that simply carried a different message in other societies.

These five fundamental conditions created a society of segments, each presuming autonomy in its domain, each requiring homogeneity of its membership, and each demanding the right to fulfill its destiny without interference. They wrought this pattern of compartments through a complex process of interaction and reinforcement. Cultural diversity separated the units of society so effectively because military security and a thin institutional overlay invited its influence, open land provided it with an appropriate setting, and abundance underwrote its indulgence; an institutional framework gave these units so much latitude because space stretched its span, security justified its looseness, cultural particularism softened its discipline, and abundance promised it a steady flow of returns; and thus from any vantage point they joined. This interweaving was neither simple nor self-evident. Institutional diffusion, for example, did not lessen fears of a centralizing power any more than military security removed those of an enemy looming outside. What these five strands did produce was a broad foundation delimiting the kind of system that Americans could construct.

The primary segments in the eighteenth century were clusters of likemindedness that defined and ordered their members from an assumption of the permanence of their family networks, religious and political practices, and social stratification. Their appropriate realms of autonomy ranged from a patrician elite's presumption of control over state government to a Baptist congregation's demand for the inviolability of its church. In the nineteenth century, communities became specific territories whose boundaries in a mobile society were protected by readily applicable standards of appearance and behavior and whose autonomy included the freedom to extend local values and local enterprise as far outward as their merit allowed. In the twentieth century, most successful Americans reshaped their primary segments around occupational privileges, determined membership according to the peculiarities each group attributed to its specialty, and claimed a predictable economic return as a fundamental right. Because large numbers of less successful Americans either modified or defied these standards through an attachment to particular places or cultural values that were irrelevant to an occupational system, the national collection of these segments displayed an intricate pattern of gaps and tiers.

Especially in the nineteenth and twentieth centuries, American society granted individuals considerable leeway, and the process of disciplining them to a system of compartments, therefore, marked one strong line of tension. Not only did segmentation leave a good many vacant spaces for individual initiative, but the importance of mobility, both geographical and social, simultaneously limited the restraints an American scheme would tolerate. In a society on the move, it was always convenient and at times imperative to rivet the responsibility for people's actions inside the individual. The very starkness of that responsibility, however, made individuals highly receptive to the comforts of a homogeneous compartment, where in the company of others just like themselves they could implicitly transfer some of the burdens of decision to a collective conscience. As David Grimsted has noted, nineteenth-century Americans expected their internalized absolutes to render precisely the judgments of their communities. Even that vaunted spokesman for the individual, Ralph Waldo Emerson, routinely fulfilled whatever tasks the Concord town meeting assigned him and vigorously defended its traditional ways against young skeptics. Throughout the nineteenth century, rootlessness was considered a morally dangerous, a personally desperate state for the individual. Twentieth-century society managed these strains in a very different manner by allocating broader and broader areas of subsidiary individual freedom. While people were expected to devote their primary energies to an occupation according to the rules it had established, they were increasingly released in another portion of their lives, apart from work, to explore the pleasures of gambling or sex or alcohol or a host of milder pursuits as they chose. Like the annual vacation, individual freedom in the secondary aspects of life, scheduled and segregated, would help to maintain group controls in its major realm.

American society guided its mobile individuals from segment to segment, not around or beyond them. The basic rights of a group—religious liberty, moral autonomy, academic freedom—became the crimes of any individual who demanded a personal version of them. If the hypothetical individual—sinful man, citizen of the republic, economic man—was a commonplace in American discourse, that terminology was used in the service of conformity, not individual freedom. In spite of their countless words on the subject, Americans contributed almost no creative thought to the meaning of the individual—the kind of insights they had, for example, into such collective activities as the church congregation, the corporation, and the administrative structure. What sympathetic attention the individual did receive concentrated largely on repairing damage, as in the activities of the American Civil Liberties Union. Individual life and welfare held low priority in a society where avid enterprise brought innumerable hazards and where surplus wealth went slowly, belatedly to such purposes as retirement income, disability insurance, and public medical service. Individuals either belonged in a category—family, community, occupation—or they really had no legitimate place at all. In America, individuals asserted themselves at a notably high risk.

During major social transitions—at the beginning of the nineteenth century and again at the beginning of the twentieth—segmentation experienced strains from the opposite direction, ones that tried to draw people into systems of loyalty much broader than the compartment. In each period an enthusiastic minority, responding to a heady sense of emancipation from the past, called for a new American consciousness to suit the new era. Following the War of 1812, they broadcast an exuberant nationalism and organized ambitious interdenominational reform associations, for instance, and in the early years of the twentieth century, they promised a great American community, to borrow Jean Quandt's phrase, and a nationwide commitment to scientific humanitarianism. As the new societies of the nineteenth and twentieth centuries materialized, however, these dreams dissipated. By the 1830s a rhetorical nationalism was increasingly lost among cries of community interest, state interest, occasionally sectional interest. Hopes for a systematic development of internal improvements had dissolved in a contest among particular enterprises, and collaborative reforms had deteriorated into the numerous activities of separate denominations, state confederations, or simply community choices. Around 1850, what John Higham has termed consolidation was the culmination of a process of hardening, multiplying segmentation. The same sequence then occurred in the twentieth century. As the new medical profession grew more secure, the American Medical Association's involvement with national reform dwindled. As the craft unions established their places in modern America, leadership over the American Federation of Labor declined proportionally. As farmers increasingly organized by commodity, the American Farm Bureau Federation came to be little more than a clearing house. During the second quarter of the century, a seemingly endless succession of divisions and subdivisions took place in business, government, and the professions. A mature American society meant the proliferation of segments, the sharpening of boundaries, the creation of more and more specific units, and as soon as they were able, Americans in both centuries followed this persuasion inside smaller and tighter compartmental rings.

In its everyday operations perhaps no Western society more closely approximated the sum of its parts. Yet Americans still managed to survive massive changes without breaking the critical threads of continuity or destroying their basic institutional channels—their constitutions and courts, churches and schools, political parties and economic enterprises. They built remarkably tough societies. What held Americans together was their ability to live apart. Society depended upon segmentation. From this elementary principle emerged a pattern of beliefs and behavior that was recognizably American.

# ~III~

# Liberty, Equality,
# and Segregation

IN AMERICA, LIBERTY WAS AN APPROXIMATE equivalent for the autonomy of a segment. Because its strength derived from the sanctity of compartmental rights, from the peculiarity of local ways, its natural effects since the earliest colonial times were divisive and insulating. A general statement of American liberties, therefore, required an extremely high level of abstraction, a set of principles so removed from the details of everyday life that they would not jeopardize any of the particular applications by an assortment of diverse, suspicious groups. From the eighteenth to the twentieth century, liberty as national doctrine was expressed through a series of formulas that acquired a concrete meaning only as various segments supplied it. Their phrasing was heavily negative, for the heart of their message was "Keep Out": bills of rights in the eighteenth century that denied government the power to interfere in certain critical areas of local choice; declarations in the nineteenth century against any intrusion into those private lanes of expanding enterprise where each individual or community or company tested its intrinsic worth; claims in the twentieth century that nothing should abridge a group's right to select their neighbors or educate their children or administer their occupation. The essence of the national tradition was a defense against outsiders, and as demands echoing from the Continental Congress to the American Liberty League indicated, it warned especially of the dangers from a distant and grasping government. Even though modern Americans had lost almost all other capacity to understand the world of the eighteenth century, they could still thrill to the rhetoric of the Revolution because here at least they continued to rely upon protective abstractions as rarefied as those of their forebears.

Liberty was central to the American experience in part because so many segments enjoyed so much of it. Yet it persisted as a vital issue because perennially its future seemed so uncertain. With national standards that could make only the grossest distinctions—between natives and immigrants, for example, or between the educated and the unschooled—Americans had to draw upon their immediate resources to identify and preserve fundamental rights that they could not expect to secure in a wider setting. If from afar a white Protestant haze covered most of nineteenth-century America, that climate did not help in making the crucial separation between one community and the next. If from below, a national elite in the twentieth century appeared a monolith of smugness and power, the occupational groups themselves not only disagreed over the measure of one another's prestige but often failed to find the common assumptions to debate it. The normal American response to uncertainty was to ally with the most exclusive available segment and pay as little attention as possible to the mass of compartments around it. Precisely because Americans lacked what Daniel Boorstin has called "givenness"—an atmospheric sense of society so pervasive no one need articulate it—liberty remained a precious commodity to seize and hoard, something people clutched to

themselves in a land where every group had a right to autonomy in spite of their neighbors. In America liberty adopted
an adversary stance. "Strange as it may seem," an astute Thaddeus Stevens wrote in 1850, "the cause of liberty is hard to
sustain in this republic. Men with difficulty understand why
others than themselves should be free."

Eighteenth-century Americans assumed that in a properly
ordered world they would be left alone inside their appropriate spheres—a church congregation, a town, a kinship network of farms and local governance, a colonial legislature.
The only conflicts they were prepared to encounter, however
odious the prospect, were the ones occurring within a segment. These their customs taught them to manage, and when
their differences grew intolerable, they could accept a solution through separation. Then congregations would divide,
communities split, or families part to form new units, each
group committed to the preservation of its distinctive beliefs
and habits and privileges and each frozen in the conviction
that its course was the truly traditional one. The same customs, the same logic reluctantly but doggedly pursued, turned
colonists into revolutionaries.

At the far end of this process, the issues of liberty began.
Almost always they focused on some external agent that was
refusing to acknowledge or actually violating the fundamentals of a community. Liberty, in other words, marked a place
along the scale of grievances where matters too basic to question had been touched. It spoke of worlds at odds—a Congre-
gational establishment challenging Baptist salvation, a distant
British government ignoring the prerogatives of Virginia gen-
tlemen—and it called compatriots to battle, not to conference.
Although these declarations were phrased in the language of
self-evidence, of rights so elementary that all reasonable people would immediately recognize them, they nevertheless signaled the presence of differences that in their present state

defied resolution. Resolutions required common ground; contests over liberty announced it did not exist. Hence the use of liberty was a solemn tactic, even if some raised it thoughtlessly, for the word involved feelings as crucial as the name of the Lord in a New England church—at times the very same feelings.

Across any wide stretch, the keenly sensed differences that separated eighteenth-century Americans in their enclaves made an inclusive statement on liberty extremely hazardous, especially if it even hinted at prescribing local ways. For general purposes, therefore, liberty was construed as absolute delegations of authority. They usually appeared as lists or bills of prohibition, formal negations such as the first ten amendments to the Constitution by which a government divested itself forever of the power to intrude. A perfected framework of these disavowals—pure liberty—meant that no outside force of any sort could disarm a community or destroy its church or disrupt its justice or dictate to its press. Never would the concept of a neutral government have such cardinal importance as it did in the area of community self-determination during the late eighteenth century. Following the extraordinary range of threats to liberty during the era of the Revolution, only a government that stood guard over compartment autonomy, scrupulously avoiding interference in its everyday affairs, could expect to command national loyalties. Both Federalists and Republicans had to relearn this lesson at the price of sharp losses in public support.

During the nineteenth century the circumstances defining liberty changed in two basic ways. As countless American enterprises ran a messy pattern of paths throughout the nation, rights that had only been carried home during the eighteenth century became matters of export. Liberty now included the protection of these outward thrusts. To serve a society based on parallel channels of growth, a minor theme of the eighteenth century came in the nineteenth to dominate the conception of liberty: for any unit—individual, community, company, region—liberty stopped just at the point where any further expansion would interfere with a comparable unit's freedom of action. Because the extent of these ambitions usually exceeded the scope of a local group's day-to-day surveillance, Americans also demanded a new and increasingly complicated range of services from both the legislatures and the courts. Rather than merely the overseers of rigid rules, they were to act as the unit's retainers, its agents of defense against intrusion anywhere along the walls that bounded its path of development. This formula, inherently imprecise in a society of grand, vague, changing schemes, was no less absolute to nineteenth-century Americans than the bills of immutable principle had been in the eighteenth century. It established a fixed point of reference in the ceaseless scramble for success, a common hope that the law could be turned to one's own advantage. If liberty in the nineteenth century was a metaphysical nightmare, it still expressed quite clearly the American prerequisites of separation and autonomy in a dynamic world of enterprise.

Liberty continued to cover the traditional realm of cultural autonomy at home, and here also the nineteenth century brought basic changes. As Americans moved from place to place, they eroded the assumptions of permanence in membership, belief, and procedure that had underpinned the eighteenth-century community, and forced the creation of new standards in appearance and public habit to guide the nineteenth-century community. Yet mobility perpetually altered a community's composition, and with a changing membership went gradually shifting rules for the regulation of local life. At any moment the community standards were absolute; over time the absolute subtly varied. The transformation of the *a priori* community of the eighteenth century into the *ad hoc* community of the nineteenth, in other words, placed a new, critical emphasis upon the collaborative capacities of a chance collection of people, upon the ability of those who happened to be neighbors to set and enforce rules in response to the circumstances of a fluid world.

The most striking consequence of these new requirements was the emergence of an American egalitarianism. The meaning of a community's homogeneity now lay on the surface of its life. Where uniform daily behavior demonstrated the very existence of community, the public act of treating everyone the same simultaneously expressed and validated its fundamentals. An easy, informal exchange among members helped to hold people's behavior in public view, exposing their differences and reinforcing their similarities. It served as a ritual of reassurance, a mundane verification that sufficient mutual trust prevailed to maintain the community's operations. Although this egalitarian veneer did not affect a host of distinctions underneath, it was remarkable enough on its own level to amaze almost every visitor from abroad by the 1830s.

Logically as well as historically, liberty preceded equality: first autonomy, then homogeneity. People would only treat each other as equals to the degree that everyone they met carried a guarantee of sameness. In a mobile society, therefore, the prerequisite for egalitarianism was an effective screening and assimilation of new arrivals. A tourist such as Alexis de Tocqueville who marveled at these egalitarian exchanges was received so openly because, as a transient rather than a prospective member, he threatened no one. A surface respectability and a short visa, in effect, qualified the passerby for the heartiest American style. The critical tasks involved sorting and policing those who might stay. Some could be barred at a glance—by skin color, by outlandish dress or manner. Others were excluded after a cursory examination, and if the community was sufficiently sturdy, they would be driven from its territory. The remainder encountered an insistent, highly utilitarian friendliness, simultaneously a quest for information and a means of communicating local ways. Reluctant responses implied resistance; reservations at best meant probation. Where so many came and went and so much depended upon homogeneity, members demanded a rapid, complete assimilation, and they consciously placed a faltering newcomer under severe stress.

Nothing about the process of community protection in the nineteenth century was either placid or routine. Particularly along the routes of highest mobility, those who preserved the community's core might well constitute a minority in a flowing sea of strangers and temporary residents. Appropriately, community anxieties often appeared in visions of inundation, a flood of aliens who would obliterate a settlement's distinctive virtue, and confidence about the future required an image of potential danger arriving in trickles. "So long as the Roman Catholic emigrants *become dispersed* among us," wrote a leader of Jacksonville, Illinois, in 1843, "I have no sort of fear, if Protestant Christians do their duty." A siege mentality was not at all unreasonable, nor were the ritual purgings of distant foes—the exorcism of a midwestern town through attacks on Utah Mormons or New York City immigrants. In fact, the ceremonial destruction of outsiders provided a rough index to the voting patterns of the nineteenth century. The inevitable need to adjust community values in response to a changing membership only accentuated the tendency to apply the code of the moment harshly and absolutely. As Jane Addams' stepmother discovered when she first arrived in Cedarville, Illinois, even a slight deviation from the current local standards in entertainment and home furnishings could rouse resentment. "No one who has not been up against it can imagine the tyranny of a small town in America," John Jay Chapman declared from the safety of Columbia University. "I believe good old fashioned Medicean, or Papal, or Austrian tyranny is child's play compared to it."

Women bore much of the responsibility for community protection. In contrast to the traditional, evolving ways of the eighteenth century, the nineteenth-century community assigned women a specific sphere of competence, one that followed the outlines of the new concern over mobility. As their primary charge, women cared for the home, where they prepared their children's character in anticipation of their ultimate departure and generally maintained a reservoir of moral strength for the family's test in the wider world. While men calculated the roads to success, women preserved the resources to travel them. Their moral realm usually extended into the community's educational and religious activities and therefore came to encompass much of its everyday involvements with homogeneity. Both an initial winnowing and a daily policing relied heavily upon observations of cleanliness and piety, family habits and personal traits, that tended to lie within this broad sphere, and many of the warnings and hints that shaped the ways of community behavior passed from wife to wife. In the eighteenth century, as families lived together over the years, men more than women had evaluated the quality of their neighbors' beliefs or the state of their characters. Now in a society of larger, fluctuating settlements and quick assessments, women more than men managed the community's internal security system.

Expanding ambitions and perpetual mobility made the nineteenth-century community, unlike its eighteenth-century counterpart, deeply, steadily dependent upon links with the outside world. Its editors and politicians—spokesmen to society at large—won their highest reward for the channels of opportunity they could build into that wider world. Churches, lodges, and labor unions were particularly prized if they gave character references to departing members and received similar credentials from new arrivals. Nevertheless, for every institution with outside connections, the price for local acceptance was a repeated acknowledgement of local sover-

eignty. The first commandment of a successful church, either
Protestant or Catholic, was an adaptation to local peculiarities. Public schools bent to the needs of the locality in both
their means of instruction and their annual schedules. News-
papers monotonously glorified local values. A political party
that tried to impose an alien cause became the enemy. Above
all, communities demanded local control in translating state
and national laws. Their version of the adage "self-government is better than good government" was simply an equation
of the two. Where each community considered itself both
distinctive and homogeneous, only a local citizen could qualify as the interpreter of distant laws, a rule that held the
placeless, faceless bureaucrat, already so familiar in Europe,
on the far edges of American society. When legislation did
force its way into a community, it violated liberty. Liberty
even above union was John C. Calhoun's reflexive reply to
Andrew Jackson in 1830, just as northern states in the 1850s
met the Fugitive Slave Act under the banner of Liberty Laws.
Only in attempting to tame the corporation did the communities eventually fail, and even here community resistance
kept the issue very much in doubt until the last quarter of the
century.

Although the basic meaning of liberty remained much the
same in the twentieth century, its applications became far
more diverse and complicated. The first critical changes came
in the lives of the new national elite who by the 1920s had
severed the intimate, traditional connection between work
and home. Elite males, defined by the functions they performed in an urban-industrial system, now depended upon
jobs for their self-respect, their reputation, and their calculations of success. Their center of liberty, therefore, was the
occupational segment, and they defended its autonomy with
the same tenacity that had once protected the community.
Prospective members were screened and indoctrinated
through the elaborate processes of professionalization, the

intricate promotional ladders of the corporation or firm, and the range of associations, fraternities, lunches, and agreements that developed to serve the needs of various businesses. Intrusions from any outside agency were countered with the grimness and resourcefulness that the very foundations of a life merited. Once again, government responded by distributing the power of self-determination to these segments as soon as they grew strong enough to demand their new rights. As in the nineteenth century, autonomy led to homogeneity and homogeneity to an approximate equality among insiders. Where the boundaries were firm, where compartmental security guaranteed a prior test for sameness, a singularly American casualness continued to prevail, as the cacophony of first names at any business or professional meeting illustrated.

Women inherited the residential portion of this division between work and home. Although it might have appeared no more than a variation of their nineteenth-century domestic sphere, that sphere had actually undergone profound changes. The nineteenth-century community, a collection of families, had relied heavily upon women for its maintenance. Each family, in turn, had been judged by a composite of its qualities, and while its reputation carried a male name, no one would have thought to question the woman's inextricable contribution to that judgment. The modern functional system not only separated residence and work but sharply subordinated home to occupation. Men now earned the family's success in some downtown office and brought the consequences back home, where they expected a house and wife and children to reflect but not materially affect these results. A wife's occasional parties and public displays were anemic substitutes for a daily involvement in the household's ranking. Increasingly men could just leave their families, if they chose, without significantly hampering their careers. With declining relevance in a male realm came expanding assumptions of female ignorance. Wives were presumed simply not to understand their husbands' world of work, a world that acquired in the process a hard masculine cast. Because character and common sense had been the standard prerequisites for almost any task in the nineteenth century, even the stereotyped southern lady, as Anne Scott has shown, could manage a variety of occupations in a time of need without excessive fuss on anyone's part and without ceasing to be a southern lady. When women entered the specialized male segments of the twentieth century, however, they were usually expected to divest themselves of all ostensibly feminine characteristics, to blend as indistinguishably as possible with their male colleagues on exclusively masculine terms. For several decades after 1910, proportionately fewer women ran that gauntlet.

The residential areas that men left behind became a new kind of woman's world. By the 1920s an increasing emancipation from household tasks and a personal mobility through automobiles and public transportation had opened a whole domain for women to explore and conquer. During the daytime hours, what men called bedroom towns were uniquely female provinces, and beneath a surface of male administration, they extended their control over the family's consumption, the locality's cultural standards, much of the town's political affairs, and above all their own right to move and behave with a freedom that their grandmothers could never have imagined. In this realm women now defined the meaning of liberty and developed a distinctive egalitarian style, as the interchangeable mothers at interchangeable doors across stretches of common yard illustrated. Elite women, in other words, built segments of their own.

In time, however, the freshness of the new freedom faded. The usual base for a wife remained the family, and lacking a central place in the system of occupational functions, the elite family continued over the decades to diminish both in importance and in cohesion. Although that decline obviously distressed many Americans, it neither disturbed the operations of the elite system nor inspired countermovements any more impressive than the pious invocations of tradition and the earnest calls for togetherness. As the lives of the elite became increasingly fragmented into discrete, expert functions, women found themselves more and more dependent in the rearing of their children on the skills of pediatricians, child psychologists, and educational specialists who claimed wisdom where mother had once been sovereign. Their instructions contained particularly sharp warnings about the psychic danger of an enduring emotional bond between mother and children, the kind that trapped children in an Oedipus Complex, held them by a "Silver Cord," generated the maudlin sickness of "Momism." In the nineteenth century, such a primary, lifelong attachment had been considered normal. As the Swedish visitor Fredrika Bremer had astutely noted about the model American husband of the mid-nineteenth century, "In every woman he respects his own mother." For elite women in the twentieth century, however, child-rearing was management, with a calculated snipping of ties as one of its major requirements. Women's traditional, reliable sources of personal gratification were shrinking. No longer was anything in family life natural or eternal; now it all had to be learned, usually from male authorities.

That same sense of living by man-made rules gave an increasingly arbitrary cast to the restrictions on women in business and the professions. In the absolute, unitary world of the nineteenth century, any woman who demanded a free choice of occupations had been required, in effect, to redesign the universe. The spheres of men and women, partaking of the eternal verities, had derived from the essence of male and female character, and reformers had found it necessary either to place their arguments on the highest ground of abstract human rights or to struggle for quite limited extensions of a female sphere. A more general mingling of men and women had attacked the fundamentals of an entire, holistic system

—a truly radical enterprise. But in the twentieth-century world of parcelled functions, each justified by its distinctive skills and each underwritten by its members' own code, the bars against women could come only from custom—a flimsy rationale for almost anything—or simple male fiat. Men, not God or nature, held them in compartments that men themselves often belittled as shallow and inconsequential. What the assaults of the 1960s and 1970s revealed was the softness inherent in a scheme of barriers that elite males could only justify by personal whim or private taste.

As the twentieth-century system of occupational functions broadened and recruited more and more auxiliaries, it multiplied the number of Americans within it who felt cramped by its discipline or degraded by its evaluations of their importance. For the millions who were either marginal to its operations or excluded from them, it simply remained an alien system, a powerful, external source of their debasement. In complex ways, a great variety of Americans organized their lives around primary values that shaded or abbreviated or contradicted the fundamentals of the elite system, and in the process they remolded the meaning of liberty to serve their particular circumstances. They might define themselves by the places where they lived rather than the jobs that they held, by networks of family or friends or ethnic affiliation rather than categories of skill, by a single core of character rather than a multiplicity of roles, by the creeds of a religious or mystical truth rather than the codes of an occupation. What they sought in each instance was an enclave of difference, a small preserve in the larger system where their special values would have absolute sovereignty.

Although these many dissents constituted an American majority throughout the twentieth century, they had only one element in common: resistance. Everything else about their defensive, exclusive opposition divided them into mutually suspicious blocs. Harlem blacks and blue-collar Jews, Selma farmers and Des Moines realtors, disconsolate middle managers and harried small businessmen, Jehovah's Witnesses and Mormons, immovable residents of Appalachia and of Berkeley, California—an extraordinary range of major and minor deviations—spread in a fanning effect around a central point of reference, the nationally visible elite standard. In the twentieth century the incessant clashes over values resembled the cries of a large mixed audience engaging a panel in many simultaneous debates. If members of the audience happened to hear an argument they liked elsewhere in the room, they turned for a moment to add their support. Usually, however, they were too preoccupied with their own cause to listen, and the din always made it difficult to follow someone else's voice. The panel seldom heard more than a snatch of complaint at a time, often nothing but noise, and it tended to regard the whole affair as a holiday for feverish minds, certainly an unfortunate distraction from the main business of life.

Among the most popular targets of this widespread, diffuse opposition was the concept of predictability, a principle that prevailed throughout the elite scheme. At the elite occupational levels where data could be systematically gathered and processed, it made sense to assume that an orderly accumulation and assessment of information could establish a verifiable probability about the future, and that results in one area could then be transferred to a comparable area. But the rationality of the computer remained irrelevant in the lives of countless individuals who continued to demand a personal mastery over the same complexity of variables. They relied instead on a special understanding of idiosyncratic events and extraordinary insights. For example, many modern dreams of success started with the realistic premise that only a miraculous intervention could place ordinary citizens in the highest reaches of American society. Character in the nineteenth-century sense would no longer help; a leap to the top now, unlike that of Cinderella or a Horatio Alger hero, seemed to require a repudiation of everyday values, a rejection of the prudential maxims in favor of Hollywood promiscuity or Jet Set extravagance. Education, connections, social polish marked an upward route that either began at birth or rarely proceeded very far. Only the defiance of prohibitive odds held real promise, and from the corner numbers game and the racetrack to Las Vegas and the stock market, modern America provided a variety of convenient outlets for the irrational plunge. Because the gambling arenas were so readily available and loosely regulated, these basic differences over chance and probability involved very little conflict. As in the case of those stubborn folk who claimed that Madison Avenue's manipulation of public behavior could never affect their impenetrable free will, such illusions actually eased social tensions by dispersing emotions into many little private cubbies.

A more direct clash of values centered on the expert. No one more clearly symbolized the gap between ordinary and elite lives than the professional specialist passing incomprehensible judgments from a cool and distant prominence. For a great many Americans, to doubt these skills was to return an element of humanity to their world, to reintegrate some of life's fragments under their personal control. Because few Americans could break totally from their dependence on expert decisions, resistance to the specialists had a notably impulsive, often contradictory quality. It rallied clients of modern dentistry against the fluoridation of their water or led supporters of the Apollo flights to link unseasonable rains with a moon walk. It gave astrology and its kindred mysteries a steady mass constituency even among those who calculated most of their affairs by another logic, and it maintained a thriving underground industry of elixirs and cancer cures. Above all, it built into American society a latent, anticipatory skepticism that exploded into laughter or anger whenever the experts bungled. A large majority wanted the specialists in at least some field to fail, thus relinquishing their sources of wisdom to each citizen's common sense and private choice.

The harshest conflicts over values—the ones with the best organized, most purposeful opposition—came in a broad realm of morals. With fewer qualifications each decade, an elite male could adopt any code of behavior away from the job that did not inhibit his occupational effectiveness. What he did and how he did it were his private affairs, just as long as they remained private. At the height of the Cold War, homosexuals were banned from sensitive government service not on moral but on functional grounds: susceptibility to blackmail made them poor "risks." By similar reasoning, Edward Kennedy was widely criticized in elite circles not for the human implications of Mary Jo Kopechne's death at Chappaquiddick in 1968 but for the poor managerial skills he displayed in handling it. Charges that Ambassador Arthur K. Watson flew drunk to a major European mission brought a standard elite reply from President Richard Nixon: "The best test of that, and I should know, is how the negotiations are going. They are going very well. Mr. Watson is conducting them with great competence and, I understand, total sobriety." Around 1970, when a greater diversity in personal styles—beard or no beard, bra or no bra—increasingly penetrated the elite offices themselves, it merely extended the basic principle that function dominated form. Only the requirements of the task exercised a logical control over elite behavior.

Large numbers of Americans either refused to accept values that divided work and leisure or resisted certain implications of the split. Codes of dress and decorum did matter for their own sake, and schools should instill these principles at least as rigorously as the ABCs. The liberal, vaguely ethical Protestantism suitable to an elite world horrified many of them, and they looked to their religion for strict guidance in a permissive society. Woman's place was in the home even if economic need might require her to take a job, and talk of female self-fulfillment would only lure the family to its destruction. Sex was a private act for procreation, and a man such as Alfred Kinsey, who spread its curious variety before the public, was simply a purveyor of filth. Around these pillars—the morals of youth, the Bible, the family, and sex—an exceptional range of Americans gathered to save themselves and their society from moral rot. While neither coordinated nor even in agreement on the causes and cures of decay, they used these issues to organize hard pockets of defense—church alliances, school groups, leagues of decency, and the like—which made them formidable antagonists in thousands of localities across the nation.

The meaning of these encounters lay less in the specific issues of public policy than in the conceptions behind it. Through their confusion of charges, opponents were arguing that the elite framework was not just askew but fundamentally wrong. When they spoke of the nation's disintegrating moral fiber, they meant something qualitatively different than the elite did when they used such terms as waste, inefficiency, and disorganization. Their political economy incorporated ways of life, patterns of behavior that penetrated the schools and churches and living rooms as well as the offices and factories. Particularly where work brought scant prestige and limited rewards, what occurred immediately around the home might represent the sole hope for a good life. Reading bad books and seeing bad movies were not private freedoms; they were public sins. A pregnant schoolgirl was an inherent disgrace, not a problem to solve, and free abortions made a mockery of that parental feeling, however welcome they might be for the daughter. Even committed anti-Communists among the elite could seldom sense the passionate yearning for a whole life behind such a slogan as "Better Dead Than Red." The few spokesmen for these dissenters who managed to find a national forum—Father Charles Coughlin in the 1930s, for example, or Governor George Wallace in the 1960s —seemed always the demagogue in elite circles, always the distraction from real issues. But to millions of Americans their blunt, simple moral judgments were themselves reality, and a Bible Amendment expressed it better than a balanced budget.

During the first quarter of the twentieth century most national leaders, after the fashion of Theodore Roosevelt, had expected public policy to integrate a modern rationality and a traditional morality, and this approach had culminated with a nationwide prohibition on liquor, which was heralded as the source for both a new efficiency and a true virtue. But widespread elite disenchantment with prohibition after the mid-twenties forced a clarification of priorities: where traditional morality interfered with modern rationality, rationality would prevail. The end of national prohibition marked an elite judgment of inconsequence, a sloughing of impediments that, in retrospect, elite spokesmen scarcely believed any sensible person could ever have sponsored. For a time this basic misconception produced a workable compromise. Out of their indifference, elites left moral policing to the discretion of local constituencies; out of their conviction, various opponents seized this power as crucial to their local lives. Those who cared understood what was happening far better than those who were now preoccupied with broad public policies. "In any hierarchy," Stanley Diamond and Edward Nell have suggested, "the lower tends to perceive the higher more accurately than the higher does the lower," an hypothesis neatly suited to these growing differences over the substance of liberty in modern America. Except for an occasional dream of national uniformity—in the heyday of Joseph McCarthy, for instance—dissenters concentrated on building and preserving their local bastions. Around mid-century a new crisis occurred only when members of the elite decided to eliminate what they now regarded as vestiges of an obsolete cultural absolutism.

During the years of compromise, more and more of these separate paths to liberty intersected in the modern suburbs.

Elites had first populated them in order to express their social standing and have ready access to the cities where they worked and enjoyed their new freedom in recreation. Unlike the standard nineteenth-century community, which had mingled people with a variety of occupations and incomes, the new suburb tended to attract residents with the same daily schedule and ambitions and educational levels. Elite families moved easily from one select suburb to another as more or less equivalent settings for their more or less equivalent patterns of living. Unlike the exclusive suburbs of the nineteenth century, where the very wealthy had lived without losing an intimate social connection to the larger city, their modern counterparts marked a separation from the city, which now served only as a location for work and pleasure.

The suburban ideal of the less successful usually represented another kind of departure from the city, a joyous escape to some safe place where people might still construct a whole life combining the right people, the right values, and the right institutions. While they also used the city for work and recreation, they much more commonly looked upon the suburban home as a fulfillment rather than an expression, as the core of their world rather than merely one appropriate piece in a larger picture. Of course, the particular values they brought to the suburbs varied just as the groups themselves varied. The great surge to the suburbs after the Second World War, in other words, told of diversity, not uniformity in the American dream. Instead of new arrivals simply emulating those who had preceded them, many types of people were chasing their different goals in the same busy circles around the city. When elites tried to establish national policy in race relations, that hidden diversity would dramatically reveal itself.

Because liberty and equality were primary American values, fraternity was not. Equality prevailed only inside a well-protected unit with a firm feeling for its distinctiveness, and

distinctiveness meant a cultivated sensitivity to alien characteristics in the wider world. In order to make sense out of the
multiplicity of undesirable alternatives surrounding them,
Americans as a matter of course developed standards by which
they could calculate the degrees of danger inherent in various
flawed beliefs and lesser people. Around each segment appeared an array of groups who were not simply different but
also inferior in some critical way—morally, genetically, ideo-
logically, educationally. The first corollary of liberty and
equality within was a systematic inequality without. Although dreams of brotherhood affected a portion of the revolutionary generation, recurred sporadically among some uto-
pians, abolitionists, and populists in the nineteenth century,
and returned after the Second World War to influence certain
strains of liberalism and radicalism, they drifted along the
periphery of a society whose organizing principles were fundamentally hostile to fraternity.

The most pervasive and enduring measures of difference
in American society were in a broad sense ethnic. Even in the
eighteenth century, when constructs of national culture were
subsidiary to issues of belief, nationality offered a convenient
means of identifying categories of people in the larger society.
The Scotch were labeled as such even though their Presby-
terianism and their attitudes toward the Revolution might
supply the basis for their reputation. In troubled times, a
strange language alone made the Germans of Pennsylvania
more suspect to many Anglo-Americans. If Federalists hated
the Irish as probable Jacobins, they nevertheless tried to exclude and deport them as Irish.

The shift from inner convictions to outward appearances,
combined with the greater specificity of European nationalism after the Napoleonic wars, elevated a secondary device to
a primary test and gave the nineteenth century its distinctiveness as the age of ethnic awareness. Because eighteenth-century usage had established nationality groupings as a reason-

able way of differentiating people, Americans could turn
easily to them early in the nineteenth century as they rebuilt
their society. The increasing diversity of immigration and
the standard insularity of community life, by accentuating
the nation's heterogeneity, steadily reinforced the utility of
ethnic standards and made them seem natural, inevitable—the
way God and history had sorted the human race. By itself, the
periodic public clamor over ethnic dangers offered a poor
guide to nineteenth-century values. The Know-Nothing
movement spread in the 1850s because the consciousness behind it had already been fixed across the nation by the 1830s.
The critical source of nativism was not the flood of Irish and
Germans during the 1840s and 1850s or southern and eastern
Europeans after 1880 but the set of the society receiving
them, the basic beliefs and customary ways of organizing life
that conditioned other Americans to perceive these newcomers in a particular manner. Similarly, the occasional drives
for national legislation to restrict immigration merely expressed a choice among techniques, one of several lines of
defense. At other times less visible yet equally rigorous devices—especially the normal protections of the community—
served well enough.

The forms of organization around an ethnic standard
varied immensely in the nineteenth century according to
the chance collections of people, their circumstances, and
their power. City life in particular made firm, dependable
communities extremely difficult to maintain, especially for
the struggling newcomers either from abroad or from the
countryside, and ethnic consciousness there tended to be
most acute, alert, and combustible. Rural communities with
a regular, heavy turnover of members might alter their ethnic
standard, however imperceptibly, almost year by year. Yet in
every setting the line between acceptable and unacceptable
at some point ran hard, and all those who crossed it to stay
were expected to divest themselves rapidly, completely of all

traits that a current absolute judged alien. The essence of assimilation in the nineteenth century was invisibility. Although the Melting Pot, always producing the same ore from any mix of ingredients, became a public issue early in the twentieth century when it was expected to homogenize whole cities or perhaps an entire nation, it was a nineteenth-century image, expressing an ideal that many communities never achieved but that all of them sought.

In a century when every way of life was presumed either to grow or to die, the implications of ethnic diversity extended well beyond the boundaries of the community. Contradictions could not exist side by side forever in a dynamic, ultimately monistic world. As Edward Beecher said of the conflict he saw between Catholicism and American democracy, "The systems are diametrically opposed: one must and will exterminate the other." During periods of high confidence, communities simply predicted the inevitable spread of their own values, the inevitable disappearance of their opponents. More often, however, they watched the wider society with suspicious attention. If the Protestant missionary impulse of the nineteenth century contained an important component of noblesse oblige, it also included a powerful urge to arm the forces of virtue in an unavoidable war with evil. Missions to the West and the cities were voluntary aid for an irrepressible conflict. Any congestion of aliens was particularly disturbing to nineteenth-century Americans. When they had faith in the digestive capacities of the community, they encouraged dispersal—the distribution of immigrants throughout the countryside—on the assumption that the osmosis of superior values into their inferior cultures would work its magic by ones and twos. But most threats were too general, too formidable for such an easy solution, and in the end, Americans concentrated their primary energies on sealing their compartments from the enemy.

Those in the twentieth century who continued to rely

heavily on ethnic standards in their everyday lives had much
more substantial reasons to worry. Most of them were losers
in the modern system of occupational functions, and they
recognized that high above them, a national leadership would
do almost nothing to protect their values. In the major cities
where more and more of them lived, the pace and scope of
physical mobility denied them a secure geographical base.
Through family ties, through neighbors more than neighborhoods, through storefront sects and favorite taverns and restricted unions, through local lore and a private reading of
the news for its ethnic content, they constructed their special
worlds as best they could. Urban politics assumed particular
importance. The nationality rallies, the hoopla for holidays
from St. Patrick's to Columbus Day, the elaborate attention
to ethnic balance among minor offices, the stylized foreign
greetings during a campaign, and much more demonstrated
the peculiar utility of a rich ethnic ritual as the surrogate for
community cohesion. Where local politics had once reflected
the community, it now served as a substitute for community.
In Chicago during the 1920s and early 1930s, precisely the
years when Italian-American households were scattering rapidly throughout the city, an Italian-American voting bloc
hardened to express what neighborhoods no longer could.

As the meaning of an ethnic identity and the occasions for
declaring it departed radically from nineteenth-century
standards, these changes did not move modern society toward a single Anglo-American norm. The high pride in being
Irish or Polish not only remained among a second- and third-
generation; for millions of Americans these ethnic attachments continued to define their primary loyalties. Contrary
to elite assumptions, no one combination of cultural values
constituted the true American core. Terms that an elite used
only to disparage, such as Greek-American and Italian-American, made excellent sense as neutral and accurate designa-
tions of these basic commitments. It would have been equally

appropriate to employ such alternatives as doctor-American and Jonesville-American. Not everyone of Italian extraction was an Italian-American, of course, any more than every doctor and every resident of Jonesville identified themselves through the values of a medical profession or a small town. Nevertheless, a carefully designed scheme of hyphenations— often multiple ones to express various apportionments of loyalty—provided by far the best glossary for America's culturally fragmented society.

In the transition from the nineteenth to the twentieth century, the new elite had also found traditional ethnic distinctions a valuable means of ordering their society. Not only did they make important contributions to the segregation of blacks, the restriction of immigration, and the closing of saloons, but they also wove these values into their new occupational segments. A relationship between jobs and ethnic standards that had once developed from a larger rationale of life was now superimposed upon a very different system. Although these discriminations covered a spectrum of color and nationalities, they operated with special effect against Jews, classically stereotyped as the adaptable infiltrators, whose existing positions of strength and commitments to educational achievement made many of them immediate candidates for the new elite. Anti-Semitic restrictions in private schools and universities, business and finance, medicine and law grew increasingly systematic during the first quarter of the century. When Richard Whitney, president of the New York Stock Exchange and pillar of an eastern Gentile establishment, identified pending New Deal legislation as the work of "a bunch of Jews out to get [the House of] Morgan," he was employing a blunt variation of a common elite idiom.

Yet by 1934 Whitney spoke for a declining tradition. What had been useful in a time of transition grew more and more anomalous as the new occupational compartments and their protective setting congealed. Skills, not culture, supplied the

natural standard for admission to a secure elite segment, and
a significant number of able practitioners held at the edges of
a compartment gratuitously weakened it. Jews demonstrated
this simple proposition by moving into such new areas of
opportunity as the movie industry, advertising, and specialized fields of corporate law and finance. Ethnic restrictions
were removed at uneven rates throughout the elite system.
Medicine, for example, responded more slowly than law.
Large corporations or agencies with a wide geographical scope
and highly mobile personnel offered a welcome to skills alone
that was often missing in businesses still rooted in a locale. In
general, these restrictions were lowered much more slowly
in elite suburbs, clubs, and similar settings that in a narrow
sense fell outside the job, and attitudes there continued to
send a subterranean influence back into work. Nevertheless,
by the 1930s the public standard had changed. Yesterday's acceptable public discourse slipped into a realm of slurs and in-
nuendoes. Although an abhorrence of fascist ideology un-
doubtedly hastened the process, the primary sources of
change lay elsewhere, in the logic of a maturing occupational
system. Early in the 1940s, Jews might have found a bit of
wry humor in the clearest single index to their own broaden-
ing opportunities: the dramatic decrease since the First
World War in anti-German persecutions at home. Among
the elite a whole range of ethnic sensitivities was atrophying.

A modern elite system, therefore, brought voluntary, face-
to-face ethnic pluralism. Always modified by private preju-
dices and circumscribed by the attitudes of various clients
and customers, ethnic differences were at least compatible
with the requirements of the new work segments. Just as a
nineteenth-century community had accepted many styles of
medicine or law or scholarship within its clear ethnic boundaries, so an elite segment in the twentieth century tolerated
ethnic diversity within strict professional rules. Along with
the new pluralism went a skepticism about serious ethnic in-

volvements of any sort. The closer a colleague's attachment to ethnic ways—Jewish holidays, an Italian heritage—the more suspect that person's occupational credentials became. The wrong priorities implied inferior performance. Although elite assimilation did not force people to swallow their ethnic values, as the nineteenth-century community had done, it still tended to drive them a safe distance from work.

Following the Second World War, a generation fully acculturated to an elite world came of age believing that ethnic differences were disappearing everywhere in American life because in their environment—at home, on the job—these differences were simply not visible. A glance across the nation told them that the old-fashioned means of distinguishing one group from another—their clothing and food, their language, their religious convictions, their ethnic ghettos—were either blurred or gone. By all they knew, a crusade against the last outposts of this dying past was a perfectly reasonable enterprise. A generation before, when a separation between elite values and those of other Americans first clearly appeared, alert people had continued to understand each other across the divide. In the mid-twenties, Chief Justice William Howard Taft, a Protestant, had courted Catholic support for his antiradicalism while anti-Catholics were denying Governor Alfred E. Smith's legitimacy as an American; but Taft could still grasp the reasoning of Protestant fundamentalism. By the time of John F. Kennedy's campaign for the Presidency, the gap had widened appreciably. Although elite commentators acknowledged the existence of an anti-Catholic vote, they could no longer understand it as a normal American option. Invariably they described it as primitive, pinched, warped—something less than human. The possibility of a dialogue had been lost in the chasm.

Just as the meaning of ethnic divisions lay inside a general pattern of segmentation, so the meaning of color lines lay inside the general pattern of ethnic divisions—a circle within the smaller circle. In America, the history of Africans, Indians, and East Asians—the black, the red, the yellow—followed the same broad guidelines affecting all disparaged ethnic minorities. During the 1820s and 1830s, when the oppression of blacks in and out of slavery was deepening and Indians were receiving Jacksonian America's summary justice, ethnic distinctions of all kinds were being sharpened throughout the nation. Around 1900, when a ring of Jim Crow laws was containing southern blacks and new legislation in the states along the Pacific Coast was restricting East Asians, racialism was hardening everywhere in America. When it was fashionable in the nineteenth century to assume that racial weakness would eventually eliminate blacks and Indians, a comparable reasoning predicted the disappearance of other despised groups, even the entire Catholic constituency. Later, when a reversal of the argument warned of proliferating, inferior blacks and yellows engulfing the better breeds, immigrants from southern and eastern Europe were designated as exactly the same danger for exactly the same reasons.

From inside any American compartment, human worth was granted to outsiders along a sliding scale, a gauge of that particular segment's antipathies. To diminish or deny the humanity of Africans or Indians or East Asians, therefore, suited a society where a variable humanity shaded from numerous cores of purity—full membership—to many horizons of marginality. No simple test of whiteness gave skin color a single meaning. American society was divided not into halves but into parts, into multiple centers defining a diversity of aliens, and across this range the ultimate enemy might be identified by color, nationality, religion, or ideology. Ghettos for blacks, reservations for Indians, and concentration camps for East Asians, rather than unique policies, were extreme instances of a general American characteristic: segregation, implying both exclusion and inferiority, came as a corollary to segmentation, one natural expression of its essential qualities.

Within this larger framework skin color found its special place in American society. In colonial America, red and black were synonymous with those qualities of culture that were usually considered most radically at odds with white communities. Africans and Indians were not necessarily the primary danger to a white community's integrity, but they marked the greatest social distances from white society. Even if skin color itself did not arouse horror, it blended with judgments of such a vast cultural separation that an easy intermingling within the community was almost impossible. When readily observable characteristics became the standard measure of acceptability early in the nineteenth century, skin color, already a clue to profound differences, emerged as central in its own right, as the substance of these differences and therefore as the threat to purity most fearfully avoided. Along with such secondary traits as the curl of the hair and the slant of the eyes, color provided a sovereign test that all Americans of all shades learned as part of a common heritage.

As a consequence, the floor of nineteenth-century society was almost always colored. To the extent that Indians entered white society at all, they were held at the bottom along a frontier of northern expansion and remained there in portions of the Great Plains and the Southwest. East Asians were placed there almost upon arrival along the Pacific Coast. But whenever Indians and East Asians were set in direct competition with Africans, the blacks overwhelmingly lost. Because of their greater surface dissimilarities from whites and their greater numbers, blacks filled the largest part of that base. As a spokesman for the American Colonization Society recognized without understanding, blacks in any concentration were "condemned, by the unalterable usages of society, to a state of degradation." Newcomers who appeared white automatically began a layer away from the bottom. Those with darker skins usually fought to free themselves from discrimination at the expense of blacks. Sherwood Anderson caught the gist of this grim game when he explained the special loyalty of San Antonio's Chicanos to the liberal Democrat Maury Maverick: "The Mexicans down there were not classified as white men. They were classified as Negroes in the census and other records, federal and state. Maury forced the classification of the Mexicans as white men. That's the way he got them, bought them. He restored to them a little of their self-respect." Yet the presence of blacks or other despised groups rarely enhanced the sense of a general white unity, as Jews, for example, did among many Gentiles in Nazi Germany. In America, the color line raised hopes of a white mobility, segment by segment, without contributing materially to a cohesive white society.

As long as the hierarchical assumptions of the eighteenth century survived, color discrimination had largely been subsumed within a general scheme of orders, one that simply assigned the least capacity, latitude, and responsibility to anyone occupying the bottom level. The full significance of color itself awaited a society where the members of a community regarded each other as essentially equal. The new meaning of skin color was prefigured early in the nineteenth century during New York's long debate over the franchise, when hierarchically oriented Federalists tried to retain property qualifications for all voters and proto-Jacksonians demanded instead the specific disqualification of blacks alone. Although a few northern Whigs and Republicans preserved elements of that Federalist tradition, they lost almost everywhere to an ethnically obsessed society of egalitarian communities. In a mobile society of absolute boundaries, skin color provided an irresistibly simple test with an implacable string of consequences. If assimilation required complete absorption—invisibility—then color was an insurmountable bar. Africans,

Indians, and East Asians were there, whites were here, and all must compete along parallel, insulated channels for the world's resources. Even slavery could not override the conclusion that blacks properly belonged in Africa, that the Chinese and Japanese properly belonged in Asia, and that America, as the standard phrase went, was a white man's country. No safe place to assign Indians left their ultimate extinction the sole solution. Where either-or values allowed no acceptable middle ground between separation and sameness, the fear of a color taint, an indelible mark of difference, was rational ground for panic. In an egalitarian community the step between entry and intermarriage was indeed a short one, and such sweeping terms as miscegenation, mongrelization, amalgamation or no amalgamation, stated quite accurately the nature of white fears. By a general application of these principles, white Americans stripped nineteenth-century society of any normal way station between bondage and freedom, as Carl Degler has explained, and made slavery an exceptionally brittle institution.

White losers in a twentieth-century occupational system found color equally critical to their sense of liberty. During the transition from nineteenth- to twentieth-century society, they welcomed a legal color line as a source of protection that their crumbling communities could no longer provide, and they erected additional barriers around their homes and jobs. As European immigration abruptly declined after 1914 and southern blacks, Chicanos, and Puerto Ricans flowed instead into the cities, the increasingly dispersed urban whites who still treasured an ethnic identity came to rely even more heavily upon skin color to sharpen the blurred boundaries. In one sense, therefore, the modern civil rights movement was a godsend, a focus upon the single line to which a scattering of whites could easily rally. Because the movement raised issues that were central to weaker Americans everywhere, its mobilizing powers proved extraordinary. Prosperity during the Second World War had generated a mass of urban purchasing power that after 1945 competed fiercely for scarce residential, educational, and recreational resources. Whites with meager satisfactions in their work had sought for years to buy what society did not otherwise offer them through an appropriately homogeneous domain with trees and schools and parks of their own. At the same time, those blacks who had also benefited from the recent prosperity now saw their ghettos doubly overwhelmed by rural migrants whom the new mechanical cottonpickers had suddenly dispossessed, and they too demanded more leeway, a greater access to these same resources which remained at a premium in the 1950s and early 1960s. In cities both South and North, whites and blacks collided in the areas where modern Americans of little prestige found their primary outlets: the rights and rewards of the consumer citizen.

These were distant matters to most members of a white occupational elite. Not only had their values diluted the significance of all ethnic distinctions, but the absence of any black threat to their segments made color an especially irrational barrier. Legal segregation above all seemed absurd. Their scheme of life had no use for Jim Crow toilets or drinking fountains or bus seats; their avenues to political power rarely depended upon a white ballot; their homes and schools were insulated by income levels, not racial lines. What they saw in the restlessness of the postwar years were the ill effects of an obsolete racial policy that, like all problems, could be corrected through careful management from above, and the sporadic clashes between whites and blacks during the 1950s and early 1960s only reinforced their conviction that segregation, an archaic source of disruption to an orderly society, had to be removed.

In the 1960s, elites pushed their new racial policies across the gaps of modern American society with explosive consequences. Those whites most immediately affected by the orders to open schools and voting booths and neighborhoods and jobs to blacks read these laws as a direct assault on their liberty. To share their rewards with blacks threatened to destroy the meaning of their quest, and they took refuge behind the friendly administration of local government to protect themselves against a national attack. In elite circles the previously unexamined differences between desegregation and integration also caused widespread dismay during the 1960s. Desegregation had connoted the removal of something, the disappearance of the wrong barriers. But as Peter Kellogg has demonstrated, white pioneers of the civil rights movement had always assumed that Americans held the right to select their own friends and neighbors, to maintain preserves of their own choice apart from public and occupational affairs. Integration on the job made sense as integration in the school did not, school integration as busing did not, busing as residential integration did not, residential integration as intimacy and intermarriage did not. If amalgamation had lost its absolute nineteenth-century meaning, it still represented the most sensitive end of a cultural spectrum. A growing portion of the elite, now judging innovation rather than anachronism the primary source of disruption, became increasingly cautious, resistant, and this in turn deepened the differences among mutually suspicious elite enclaves. By the end of the decade, segregationists were discovering a new range of friends and quiet allies all across the land.

As the half-hidden ethnicity of modern America erupted in the 1960s, its emotional power only verified the importance of ethnic values to those who had been defined as colored. Many Afro-Americans, Chicanos, Indians, Puerto Ricans, and East Asians interpreted their lives in ethnic terms not simply by choice; the whites around them imposed these rules of understanding. Perforce, this was their American way. Drawing upon their own ethnic resources, they discovered new means of cohesion, new reserves of pride in their unique characteristics and heritage. What had once been the clichés of white rejection—the charge, for example, that blacks really belonged in Africa—now offered strength and hope. Within its larger ethnic setting, Black Power expressed a traditional American goal—the creation of an autonomous, homogeneous unit by the most practical and available means—and its extension into dreams of a separate black nation no more than an extreme version of the same logic.

Applied to an entire society, this reasoning also sustained the myth of white unity. The claim that whites had broken a promise of integration was less than absurd only because of the more outrageous illusion among elite whites that they could make such promises. In fact, recent black history made sense only if a simple, flat white racism did not, but because most blacks were surrounded by ethnic values, they presumed the universality of these values. To a number of angry blacks, the whites who bluntly declared their allegiance to a color line had at least the saving merit of honesty, as Congresswoman Shirley Chisholm said of George Wallace and several black radicals said of the contemporary Ku Klux Klan. For similar reasons, the charges of a so-called reverse racism among blacks did have point. As they understood their world, this was how you charted its meaning and survived inside it.

Mismanagement of racial policies seriously affected an elite's power over a wide range of cultural issues. The turmoil over black rights triggered general responses among whites who for years had been accumulating resentment about a spreading pattern of outside cultural controls. This elite aggrandizement, often identified with the Supreme Court under Chief Justice Earl Warren, included new national rules in such areas as Protestant religion in the public schools, customary methods of local law enforcement, and the distribution of obscene and otherwise objectionable materials. Each of these realms by tacit understanding had fallen outside the purview of national government and therefore within a residual domain of local determination. Each change, expressing a national elite judgment, jarred a basic sense of liberty among millions who were living by very different values. As in the case of integration, these pronouncements reflected a critical elite ignorance, a delusion of managerial omnicompetence in a rapidly homogenizing America; and dissenters, along with their resistance to national policies in race, mounted an effective counterattack across a broad cultural front. Race, in other words, supplied both the catalyst and the occasion for a mass retaliation. Sharp public reactions quite severely pared the areas of cultural dominance which for decades elites had been gradually expanding. For a time, elites even had some difficulty protecting such traditional privileges as the governance of major universities and the right of their children to choose almost any style of adolescence without legal interference. The trend of the 1970s was a sharp contraction in national controls, an effort to disengage the political economy from those cultural involvements which might again disrupt the social order.

Americans elevated no value higher than peace. Not even prosperity outranked it, for peace determined whether or not American society was functioning. Its centrality lay in its peculiar definition: peace meant the absence of conflict. It did not require affection or trust or any other quality of human interaction. The object was a negative, one that proved the success of segmentation by gauging the insulation among the parts of society, and whenever the issue was in doubt, the most natural corrective was greater separation—a thousand miles between Mormons and their neighbors in the mid-nineteenth century, concentration camps for Japanese-Americans in the mid-twentieth. Minimum contact promised minimum conflict. For more than a century segregation maintained that kind of peace between whites and blacks, and only when segregation itself seemed a source of conflict was it broadly assaulted. The Civil War obsessed Americans not as an illuminator of their society but as an aberration, as an apparently unique and overwhelming loss of peace. An equally obsessive concern about cities reflected the reasonable judgment that urban life made peace, by American standards, extremely difficult to attain.

Although the number of people and size of territory that peace was expected to cover varied considerably, its connotations in each setting were absolute. It demanded total quiet. The ambiguities of a ruffled calm or an indeterminate engagement simply represented variations on conflict. Such phrases as social unrest and the immigrant problem did not describe situations to consider; they located dangers to eradicate. While peaceful coexistence was a somewhat redundant consistency, an uncertain peace was a contradiction in terms— a Cold War, as it were, demanding somebody's capitulation, some ultimate, clear resolution—and the widespread use of war as shorthand for all kinds of domestic tensions and eruptions expressed this mentality. The insistent prettiness of American popular literature, with every seam tucked and justice meted to all, was an index not to shallow minds but to social needs, to values so basic in an American scheme that their rigidity served as a measure of their significance.

Similarly strict conditions applied to the internal state of each compartment, where peace verified homogeneity. Although finer lines here distinguished the expected from the unexpected, the disputes customary to a segment from those no one anticipated, a special hatred for the troublemaker, running from the Puritans to the present, suggested how passionately anything on the wrong side of the line was received. With very few exceptions, the magnet of disturbance attracted the blame. Because peace transcended other values, challengers were judged less by an analysis of their protest than by the degree of conflict it drew. Speeches became inflammatory when disruptions followed. Striking wage-earners usually created a labor problem and dissenting college students a youth problem in quite direct ways, just as declarations of "no trouble in my factory" or "no trouble on my campus" usually carried simple messages of health quite apart from the human circumstances that surrounded them. Orderly petitions through safe channels and orderly marches along sealed routes had an appeal far beyond any desire for procedural neatness.

Different patterns of sensitivity from century to century did not seem to change the commitment to this kind of peace. The alacrity with which patricians in the late eighteenth century read hints of an unauthorized disturbance as a challenge to good order, for example, was approximately equivalent to the fearful anticipation among nineteenth-century community leaders of subversion and conspiracy in their midst. What resiliency certain types of relativism brought to a twentieth-century elite was balanced against a new national scope to their sense of danger and new consequences from the separation of home and work. Where the standard nineteenth-century community was a unitary world that had to meet whatever disputes local life generated, the divisions of the twentieth century invited evasion. The habit of assigning problems to their appropriate areas of specialization encouraged members of the elite to escape trouble by a similar sorting technique. The conflicts they encountered were always, obviously out of place and could only be managed by other people in other specialized subdivisions. The exceptional care that most American dissenters took to establish their peaceful intent—their avowals of traditional values and purposes, their manifestations of lawfulness and sobriety and patience—indicated that over two centuries they at least had anticipated a roughly common response.

Violence came as the natural accompaniment to peace. Americans were not in some visceral way a singularly violent people, given to mauling each other or besetting neighbors

or waylaying competitors. Nor did they prove peculiarly sus-
ceptible to bloody binges of irrationality, as the popular ac-
count of America's red scares in the twentieth century would
imply. Not even the publicized uses of violence to establish
manhood set Americans apart from a rich European tradition.
What particularly distinguished American violence was its
regular, normal service in behalf of an American peace.

A well-ordered community in the late eighteenth or nineteenth century seldom used violence on its own members.
Even where law or custom allowed it, such means reflected
badly on the state of local society, and as long as the power to
establish and police rules, to employ subtler forms of collective restraints, remained at a community's disposal, it
shunned measures that would imply weakness. Exceptions fell
largely into quite limited realms of community approval.
Crimes regarded as particularly heinous might justify a rare
rite of torture or execution—tar and feathers, for instance, or
lynching. Because in this setting a person's character defined
his opportunities in life, individuals had recourse to certain
violent ways of expressing their absolute denial of a serious
charge. A duel on some crucial matter of honor or the beating
of a brash newspaper editor represented a categorical public
rejection of accusations that might otherwise cripple a man's
standing where it most mattered. Yet even in these areas a
strong community presumed clear limits, and deviations
brought either direct punishment or judgments of character
that in the case of excessive dueling and caning could destroy
the very reputation an individual was seeking to preserve.

Only when a deeply disturbing crisis placed in doubt either
a community's values or its membership did these restraints
weaken. The Revolutionary process, for example, raised
cloudy questions of mutual trust that the standard community procedures could not always manage. So also during the
transitions from the eighteenth to the nineteenth and from
the nineteenth to the twentieth century, a malaise of uncer-

tain values, of muddied distinctions between friend and enemy confused the normal patterns of violence. Even then, however, the web of control seldom disappeared. Mobs of the Revolutionary and Jacksonian eras and Klan justice in the 1920s tended not only to function at first under local leaders or the community's tacit approval, but in time to raise demands for containment. The threat they posed was measured by the degree of community regulation rather than by the degree of violence. As abnormal procedure, perhaps more dangerous than the evils it was attacking, vigilante justice usually roused effective countermeasures after a flurry of activity.

Just as long as people could distinguish clearly between members and outsiders, their use of violence against invaders signified much the same community strength as their use of persuasion on each other. Protecting the community was a sacred charge, one that justified any effective deterrent if intruders ignored due warning or brought special danger. Carriers of an alien religion in the seventeenth century, agents of a foreign law in the eighteenth, and proselytizers of an immoral cause in the nineteenth received remarkably similar, abrupt treatment when they persisted in the face of community disapproval; bloodied organizers for the CIO, Jehovah's Witnesses, and civil rights in the twentieth century testified to the sturdiness of that tradition wherever hopes for an integrated community still prevailed. A common ceremony connected these acts of violence over the centuries. When citizens of Alton, Illinois, who hours later would condone the murder of the abolitionist Elijah Lovejoy, resolved in 1837 "that as . . . the friends of order, peace, and constitutional law, we regret that persons and editors from abroad have seen proper to interest themselves so conspicuously in the discussion and agitation of a question, in which our city is made the principal theatre," they varied only the style and detail of colonists in 1765 who then attacked British tax collectors, or residents of Everett, Washington, in 1919 who then fired into a boatload of Wobblies. Always the justification was a community peace that stubborn intruders had broken and that violence, in the garb of law and order, would restore.

These same values also applied to aliens who simply did not leave. Major corporations that violence could not remove stood exposed to random attack as long as they represented an alien presence. To find evidence in the communities of the Southwest around 1900 against robbers of the Southern Pacific Railroad defied the talents of the best detective. In later years the conscientious courtship of local favor by large corporations made sense, among other reasons, as an elementary insurance against property damage. Resident outsiders without power—a cluster of impoverished blacks or Indians, for instance—lived at the mercy of a community that denied them membership and therefore refused them the protection of its restraints. Mounting tensions from any source, hints of obstreperousness, personal whim—any number of errant reasons —might cause occasional violence just as long as these events did not jeopardize the fabric of community life.

In part, Americans resorted to violence because of their assumptions about the roots and range of individual morality. If behavior was controlled by the rules of the compartment, sovereign for its members and delimited by its boundaries, who could say how people at large, people cut loose from their moral base, might behave? Anyone with dubious credentials was automatically suspect, a reflection perhaps of the psychic drift everyone had experienced far from home. A presumption of amorality, of unregulated people wandering in nobody's land, quickened thoughts about violence as it removed the checks on its use: treat others as you assume they want to treat you. Such reasoning did, in fact, encourage violence among people on the loose and helped to explain why American cities were particularly dangerous places. Many acts of violence that in a European society would have expressed some connection to a broader public or political cause demonstrated the absence of those links in America, the segmented nature of its moral responsibility.

During the nineteenth century, violence as a calculated tactic altered in response to the growing emphasis on legal procedures. The more a community depended on an impersonal economic network for its opportunities, the more a formal structure of law became associated with public order. The changes over a century, while selective and gradual, were impressive. Matters of individual honor or community standing assimilated most readily into the new scheme, and duels, then beatings declined as it expanded. Considerably more complex changes occurred in community defense. As private and vigilante violence lost favor, a legally glossed violence—by the police or the militia—received increasing attention and approval. At the same time, the scope of a community's defense broadened to cover larger areas of a city or state or at critical times even quite distant places in the nation. Early in the twentieth century, the new occupational elite combined these strands into a national system that could only operate through an elaborate, generally accepted legal procedure. Inside the elite world, the informal resolution of problems by violence was now a cardinal sin, and the very prospect of violent challenges—by anarchists or Bolsheviks or saboteurs or youthful revolutionaries—became the most dangerous message of the subversive. Even the authorized violence of police and troops on a large scale implied jeopardy to a legally ordered society. At least in public discourse, violence as proper defense of a segment had been anathematized by the mid-twentieth century.

Set against such a dramatic shift in values, behavior changed relatively little. Although the elite eschewed violence in their public lives, they either justified it elsewhere instance by instance as a necessary protection against disorder or merely tolerated it around them. Weaker groups who had never pretended to disown violence employed it more circumspectly than their nineteenth-century predecessors but no less persistently to their own problems of exclusion and discipline. What explained this apparent contradiction between standards and practice had, in fact, been sustaining violence for centuries. The line of empathy in a segmented society was exceptionally short. The very sources of its strength inside a compartment, where compassion and mutual help between equals gave a certain glow to American history, also cut its length sharply at the boundary. Those outside of the compartment lost their human qualities layer by layer along descending scales that expressed each segment's primary values, and the effect was a massive insensitivity to the treatment of very different people. In immediate encounters, these perceptions greatly facilitated the use of violence against marginal people; in a larger setting, they placed such acts in a huge void. It was blankness—not bloodthirsty cheering but an overwhelming unconcern—that surrounded the massacre of Indians, the cruelty to East Asians, and the abuse of European immigrants. In the countless pockets of the nineteenth and twentieth centuries, news of inhumanities "arrives drained of urgency by the obstacles it has to cross," obstacles that were far more social than geographical.

Personalized and isolated violence often elicited strong responses that seemed for a moment to transcend these barriers. The hapless Cuban señorita of William Randolph Hearst's imagination in 1898 or the lynched black unloosed floods of feeling that never touched the abused immigrant laborers from Latin America or the ensnared black sharecroppers. The focal dread of murder gripped generations of Americans that could barely attend mass brutalities. How many movie heroes slaughtered faceless Indians or bombed cities only to prove their humanity by the dramatic remission of a single life? Whatever else these emotions expressed, they belonged to a category, not of empathy, but of the sympathy that Konrad Lorenz has described running well down the evolutionary ladder and engaging people to the degree they find human analogues, certain human likenesses, that can reach deep within them. Spontaneous and socially sterile horror over atrocities, in other words, did not conflict with the perception of millions as markedly less than human. Honest tears for a lynched black need not mean much more than equally honest tears for a dying dog.

Where empathy extended beyond the segment, it moved in narrow channels. These normally thin strands left almost no trace, and exceptions, such as the record of certain Quaker missionaries, stood as lonely curiosities. Nor did modern communication significantly alter the patterns. While students were expressing their outrage in 1970 over the murders at Kent State University, four out of five Americans were declaring their support of the killers. And the few whites who gathered in 1971 to commemorate the Kent State Four had in almost all cases forgotten their vow of a year earlier to link forever that event with the simultaneous murder of black students at Jackson State University. A segmented society dispersed its memories in little pieces.

The foundation of liberty in America was social boundaries, not human feelings, and lacking those clear boundaries, Americans could anticipate only chaos in human relations. If we let in just one, a standard sequence went, how can we stop them—Jews or blacks or Communists or uncertified professionals—from taking everything? Those males who argued in the 1960s that if women wanted legal equality they must therefore fight the wars and haul the heavy loads of their society may have ignored the innumerable distinctions that men themselves had always made in apportioning work, but they nevertheless followed a deeply traditional American logic. A single break in the line obliterated the meaning of the line. That primary commitment to securing compartmental boundaries sufficiently diffused energies during the major transitions between the eighteenth and nineteenth and the nineteenth and twentieth centuries to invest American society as a whole with a critical quality of looseness, an inner check against the broad, hard mobilization of opposing forces. By this same set of values, this same segment mentality, Americans then shaped the structure of their new societies, preserved their liberties, and maintained a fundamental continuity across the centuries.

# ~IV~

# *A Whole Society*

EACH GENERATION HAS had to rediscover America, for its meaning has been a problem that could be neither ignored nor resolved. Americans pursued it so doggedly because so much depended upon an answer. Emotions that in another country might be apportioned among an established church, a social class, and a standing challenge to national boundaries, for example, concentrated with a peculiar, lone intensity on the presence of a whole America, on the imperative of creating and sustaining elementary confidence in a cohesive national society. Yet the sources of cohesion were forever elusive. An alert visitor abroad learned promptly, as Nathaniel Hawthorne reported, that Americans "have no country—at least, none in the sense an Englishman has a country." Wells of national sentiment that Queen Victoria or Louis Napoleon or Adolf Hitler so effectively tapped simply did not exist in America. Memories, loyalties, ambitions were always too scattered. Through images of a youthful, lusty, questing nation, Americans did try to transform the looseness of their society into a virtue. But a persistent note of uneasiness running throughout American history expressed anxiety about precisely those qualities of formlessness that eternal youth connoted.

Segmentation both defined the need for cohesion and set the terms for satisfying it. It was as if each compartment, unable to hear or see clearly what lay beyond its walls, required constant reassurance that it was indeed connected with the next unit and the next and the next in a common, rewarding enterprise. Those institutions which might have facilitated access into a wider society were adapted instead to the endless variety of specific, compartmental requirements. Already in the eighteenth century most of the founding fathers took pride in the absence of a military or church or educational establishment, with distinctive traditions and experiences of its own, that would have mediated among separate elite groups. Loyalty to the political parties of the nineteenth century depended upon their compatibility with local values, and their rubbery platforms expressed this truth. In the twentieth century, those few people who wanted their new occupational segments to influence a wide range of social issues declared themselves generals without an army. From Samuel Gompers to John L. Lewis to Walter Reuther, officials who tried to translate union loyalty into broad social objectives either failed and retreated or failed and retired. Aside from the specific concerns of the profession, there was no medical interest in modern America. Technocracy was a movement without technicians. The essence of an occupational compartment was exclusiveness; to the degree it prospered, it blocked the avenues into a wider society.

Class consciousness encountered the same resistance from diversity and particularism. As Herbert Gutman has explained, wave after wave of raw laborers from the countryside and from abroad swamped each early growth of class consciousness during the nineteenth century, and a culture of working people never materialized to guide actions and interpret events wherever a laborer might live. Instead, workers fitted themselves to a scheme of compartments that merely accentuated their suspiciousness and separateness. An absence of class consciousness among wage-earners, in turn, critically influenced class consciousness elsewhere. Successful Americans rarely felt driven to join a broad movement in defense of their common interests, and even these urges were seldom prolonged. Federalist fears of Jacobinism dissolved in an eminently safe Republican regime; elite mobilizations against a class uprising late in the nineteenth century, around the First World War, and during the 1930s dwindled in each case when no formidable enemy appeared. Similarly, economic privilege early in the nineteenth century and around 1900 was simply too diffuse a foe and its effects on most Americans too ambiguous to cement a class in opposition. It would have required far more systematic and sustained dangers to resist the pulls of segmentation. America lacked social classes not because it was exceptionally united but because it was too subdivided to maintain them.

Geographical loyalties, a far more substantial part of the American heritage, also inhibited connections with a whole society. During their greatest strength in the nineteenth century, they were almost always rooted in a community, and as community ambitions drew people outward, their lines of loyalty tended to follow their lines of enterprise—sometimes to a county or a valley, more often to a state. Around midcentury when the maintenance of slavery or free soil, and of the many ambitions associated with each, seemed to demand an even broader setting, the next logical extension was sectionalism. At each stage the primary meaning of these larger frameworks was protective, a wall of security no wider than necessary to preserve the enterprises within and to intercept dangers from without. During the nineteenth century, there was nothing reactionary about these loyalties. Psychologically, jurisdictionally, a state usually represented the most appropriate agent for local projects, and a commitment to state rights was the natural supplement. Yet even in a boastful, promotional form—virtuous Massachusetts against the decadent slaveholders, the rugged West against an effete East—such loyalties generally defined differences in a way that severely hindered intercourse, that implied enemy territory on the other side. In the twentieth century, as local and state attachments lost more and more of their entrepreneurial associations, they finally did come to express quite direct negations of the dominant national system. In the abstract, as David Potter argued, these loyalties need not have been so restrictive century by century; but in America they were.

Americans looked at their society as though it lay across a stripped plain. No clear routes beckoned, no way stations invited them to come and view it from another angle. To comprehend it at all, they would have to see it flat and whole. In times of minimum stress, they responded with the sweeping assertion. John Jay, who was writing from the conglomerate city of New York in the midst of the heterogeneous middle states separating New England from the South, declared in 1787, "Providence has been pleased to give this one connected country to one united people—a people descending from the same ancestors, speaking the same language, professing the same religion . . ."; and over the next two centuries countless publicists echoed his synthetic Anglo-Saxonism. In a haze of memory, wars seemed to have been extraordinary sources of unity that rededicated a dispersed and selfish citizenry to high national purposes. Perhaps nothing served so often or so well in the nineteenth and twentieth centuries as some variant on the announcement, "We are all middle class!" Customs and habits also fed the rhetoric of national cohesion in the nineteenth: Americans were a god-fearing people, a liberty-loving people, an industrious people. These gave way more and more in the twentieth to patterns of common consumption—the omnipresent radio or TV, the mass-produced clothes or cars—and evidences of common thought—

mass media and yes-or-no opinion polls—as proof of an increasingly uniform society. Only Americans could have claimed that the internationalization of chewing gum and Coca-Cola after the Second World War meant the worldwide triumph of their culture.

Although these assertions could express confidence, they could not create it. To meet even the normal quota of doubts and fears and conflicts that a wider society bred, Americans had to rely upon the only principles at their disposal, those inherent in their compartmental lives. There the standard was a relatively simple, carefully nurtured homogeneity. The critical question, segment by segment, was in or out, and the classic problem was one of assimilation rather than accommodation, of eradicating significant differences rather than mediating among them. Above all, it was this logic of line-drawing that in their search for unity Americans applied to the society at large.

As the range of their interests broadened, Americans were highly vulnerable to a sudden, jarring contradiction between their compartment's absolute values and the diversity around them. Just beneath the soft assertions of unity lay the hard demands for conformity, the need to resolve the contradictions that they encountered by enforcing homogeneity. At the same time, the urge for unity sharply limited the means of achieving it, for a prolonged, general campaign against enemies would only verify the absence of that precious wholeness. Cohesion in a segmented society, therefore, required a high level of abstraction and a low level of implementation. And because rules as rigid as those customarily employed inside a segment would have destroyed any hope of national unity, people learned ways of shading them in behalf of a cohesive America. Sometimes an ethnic group who would never have qualified by local standards found a place, however lowly, in their national vision. Comparisons helped: the Irish were at least superior to the blacks, Jews certainly made better citizens than Italians, and so on. Ideological or educational or occupational criteria could be eased in a similar fashion to achieve maximum inclusiveness. By emphasizing the absence of intolerable people rather than the presence of desirable ones, Americans did manage to dilute the effects of a homogeneous ideal in a heterogeneous land.

But try as they might, most Americans most of the time stopped considerably short of encompassing the nation. According to their calculations of a graded humanity, the divider at some point fell: in-out. With mixtures of horror and resignation, Americans came early to accept the inevitable presence of outsiders, aliens somewhere in their land. Citizenship and membership, a relatively simple equation in France, formed the components of an exceedingly complex problem in America. Although every citizen could claim a basic set of legal rights, some of these citizens would almost certainly remain outsiders. Actual membership was determined by additional tests of religion, perhaps, or race or language or behavior, tests that varied considerably among segments and over time. Each generation passed to the next an open question of who really belonged to American society.

In that shadow land of aliens hid the conspirator. A segmented society surrounded each compartment with strangers whose values were already suspect and whose evil intent was a reasonable corollary. With power diffused among so many centers, it was extremely difficult to locate the sources of a major decision on public policy, and a blurring of the points of authority also meant obscuring any clear objects of opposition or hate. In a democracy, where the people controlled their government and established their own values and goals, what, other than a conspiracy, could explain a general change for the worse? Were the whole people corrupt or had some alien group stolen the power to set vice over virtue? Within this context, Richard Hofstadter's distinction between seeing conspiracy in history and seeing history as a conspiracy was often no more than an incremental one. The many vacuums of power in a segmented society did encourage schemes and plots. Although most of them served only narrow interests, some actually tried to move the entire society. Fundamental decisions ranging from the preparation of the Constitution to the war in Indochina raised precisely the kind of doubts that made conspiracy a reasonable explanation.

An assumption of conspiracy, in other words, was a normal American predisposition that affected people of every persuasion and temperament. Its target might be a neighboring town or international finance, a local Mason or a distant Mormon. It covered slaveholders and free soilers, industrialists and unionists, liquor interests and dry crusaders, atheists and Catholics, anarchists, socialists, fascists, and communists. Charges of conspiracy suffused American politics. They influenced every founding father. Democrats and Whigs constructed platforms upon them. When Lincoln and Douglas debated in 1858, these sober, tough-minded politicians so intermingled conspiracies small and large with matters of state that no one could disentangle the two, nor should anyone have tried. In 1898, with that model of propriety, William McKinley, in the White House, congressional Democrats took a solemn oath to defend the Constitution against a Presidential coup. First the trusts, then economic royalists, finally a military-industrial complex reputedly strung politicians like puppets, while Franklin Roosevelt's associates were allegedly stealing the nation's gold and committing "twenty years of treason." In the twentieth century a newspaper could —and many did—report a new political conspiracy every day. Substance and style changed time and again, but the basic assumption remained intact.

The predilection toward conspiracies was extremely useful in the cause of cohesion. Because people employed this mode of understanding in their everyday affairs, it did not require elaborate communications to reach a dispersed or otherwise divided population. When Harry Truman reflexively identified the early black sit-ins with Communism, millions could automatically grasp the message and apply its meaning at home, much as previous generations had responded to Monarchism and Jacobinism, Papal plots and financial cabals. A conspiracy not only accepted but actually depended upon the inevitability of outsiders within the United States, and it offered people a ready device for separating the virtuous majority from an evil few. In the process, it gave national dangers an immediacy that geography had denied them. Particularly from the 1820s to the 1930s, no power in the western hemisphere could elicit more than puffs of concern: some worries around the middle of the nineteenth century about European designs on Texas or Mexico or the Far West, occasional doubts in later years about Caribbean security, but nothing more urgent. Enemies within meant immanent jeopardy, and the sense of danger was sharpened by stories of these aliens taking their orders from a foreign master. Here, moreover, was a threat touching everyone, an American call to arms. Precisely where and how these minions operated or what resources they had at their disposal were usually left vague, and Americans could adapt the particulars, as they might a folk tale, to suit their special circumstances.

As with every other effort to create a whole America, these many applications of a common persuasion continually highlighted diversity in the quest for unity. Some versions of conspiracy did attract wide, loyal audiences and did effectively veil differences among them over many years; anti-Catholicism and anti-Communism were the most noteworthy. But no America existed in the cultural sense that people were seeking, and hence groups sharpened their own feelings of belonging by challenging each other's legitimacy. Appropriately, many of these debates in the nineteenth century narrowed into mutual charges of conspiracy: Protestant and Catholic, abolitionist and slavocrat, Populist and banker. In the twentieth century Americans increasingly talked past each other. A modern elite, blind to the popular urge for cultural cohesion and certain that the cries of a conspiracy against the Bible or the family or the white race were the ravings of stunted minds, tried instead to convince the nation that only one type of conspiracy, subversion of America's political economy, was a truly rational assumption. Century by century, these competing claims of conspiracy served as an excellent guide to the tensions between compartmental particularism at one end and the enduring need for national cohesion at the other.

Where people started determined the kind of unity they sought. From the primary qualities of their segment they made a relatively simple projection across the flat terrain before them, extended it as far as their values and temperaments would allow, and calculated the strength of the society by the fit between their overlay and their nation. They superimposed America on the United States. What shape these many visions took, how from time to time the dimly outlined, overlapping schemes that citizens had thrown across each other coincided or clashed, set the terms for the history of American cohesion.

A legacy of such visions dated back to the grand designers of the seventeenth century, Englishmen who were frustrated by their own tumultuous society and who looked to America, a blank new world, for the fulfillment of their ambitions. The plans of Puritans for Massachusetts Bay, of Lord Baltimore and William Penn for their proprietary tracts, and at a more abstract level of John Locke for the Carolinas suffered almost immediate, irreparable damage in a strange land with its own compelling demands, and settlers were left to face this American vacuum no longer as a unique hope but as a singular threat. For seventeenth-century colonists who conceived of order as stern controls over men's natural weaknesses, America's crude settlements accentuated the usual fears of chaos and forced attention to the most elementary requirements of social discipline. This turned energies inward, where within a very limited compass they could best organize the sources of security. By the late seventeenth century a multitude of small fortresses were already establishing traditions in their own right that would resist efforts to integrate them into any sort of broader system—doctrinal, political, commercial.

That unresponsiveness to a wider authority perplexed and infuriated those on both sides of the Atlantic who for various reasons sought greater coordination in colonial life. Across any broad territory—a region of settlement, a colony, a seaboard—the flow of life seemed invariably centrifugal. Charges of a peculiar American slovenliness and cantankerousness and insolence became an incessant chant, encouraging innumerable schemes to unite a dispersed, unruly people: a tightened imperial system, a revival of true doctrine and piety, an importation of courts or troops or church establishment. When reasonably persistent attempts to discipline colonial society were finally made in the 1760s and 1770s, they precipitated a revolution.

Revolution increased these responsibilities as it transferred them across the Atlantic. Presiding over an artificial union of former colonies, a revolutionary leadership not only inherited the British need to deal with all the states; it was now required to find bonds among them, to make them in some basic sense whole. Although the founding fathers hedged by calling the union no more than an experiment, and by retreating inside state or regional defenses whenever they could not exercise national power, they never entirely freed themselves from the challenge of establishing a cohesive nation. Form was an imperative in their republican enterprise. Just as they followed the particulars of constitution-making with special concentration, so they measured every detail in behavior and policy against a preconceived structure of social relationships as the critical test of the new nation's promise. Their tense concern for the purity of fundamental principles, their bitter partisan battles, their quick despair when plans went awry, all told of a wearing struggle against diversity that they could never quite escape.

The image of unity in the eighteenth century was some variation of the hierarchical pyramid that rose tier by tier from base to apex. In New England the pyramid stretched in the middle and flattened at the top, reflecting a scarcity of the very poor and considerable competition for leadership. Among the estates in New York and the plantations in the South, where renters and slaves filled the base and a single family often stood atop the structure, its middle ranges lacked the kind of clarity that the close relations of a compact New England community could give social differences. Indeed, that fuzziness in detail left many Southern patricians fretful about the very existence of an eighteenth-century community in their domains. Standards for the new nation derived from these local circumstances. Where hierarchies were reasonably precise, as in much of New England, prominent citizens expected a similar articulation in the entire nation. Where leadership was an automatic and singular prerogative, as in much of New York and Virginia, local patricians anticipated the same specificity in national affairs. And where the base of the pyramid contained a dubious mass, as in New York City and the slave-heavy sections of South Carolina, leaders demanded a national system that was equally alert to dangers from below.

These complex local interests then met in the debates over the meaning of the new nation. What gave them unusual focus was the ambition of Alexander Hamilton, presiding genius of the Federalists, to fashion nationally a society at variance with local customs. Hamilton envisaged a national society of discrete categories and protected privilege: interests emanating from a new central government would create a ruling elite of wealth and taste; a larger stratum of lieutenants would mediate between nation and locality, translating policies from above and maintaining order below; and a residual mass would prosper through obedience and industry. Three distinct blocs, interdependent yet separate. By moderating divisions and honoring local autonomy, Americans had established a proliferation of whole communities; by clarifying differences and elevating national interests, Hamilton would have detached an elite from these communities and built a national society with a special logic of its own. Visualized as an improvement on the English model, it drew strength in the northern states where aristocratic British values had won their widest currency, and it also appealed to a variety of those who welcomed precise gradations and who worried about disturbances from below.

It was a daring departure. In one sense, Hamilton's plan took its inspiration from imperial politics late in the colonial years, when a relatively small group with ties to both sides of the Atlantic had formed a cluster of interests around each governor. But its central meaning in the 1790s was innovation, a new structure independent of the countless little societies that were operating by other values. Many of these local societies would have invested no leader with the authority Hamilton and his elite required. Others who might have granted a leader these prerogatives did not share the fears of a disorderly mass, and an occasional use of force by the Federalists to implement the law and cow the obstinate conjured a picture of liberty at bay rather than order at hand. Inevitably the prospects of a separate elite suggested analogies to British rule, a dangerous association for a revolutionary generation. By setting national and local ways at odds in a society where the simple projection of community truths was already common, Hamilton's scheme even caught many Federalists in a crossfire between national service and local tradition, and whenever national policy threatened local integration, they too were required to place their community first as the price of power.

The challenge had its leader in a manner that the response did not. If the answer to Hamilton's interest blocs was Jeffersonian, it relied far less upon any man. Reflecting rather than innovating, it drew its greatest strength not from ambition but from inertia. In an artificial, heterogeneous nation, a bold departure demanded ceaseless exertions—plans, calculations, risks, reinforcements—that surpassed even Hamilton's extraordinary talents. A successful reply required above all a certain mistiness, a felicitous shading of the lines so that each community would feel a consonance between its local ways and a national society. In this respect Jefferson was an exceptionally able spokesman. By temperament he avoided—perhaps never even asked—the hard questions about system and order that Hamilton posed, answered, and pursued. He expanded upon his experiences in a loose Virginia hierarchy, with its safe layer of white farmers toward the bottom, to sketch broad unities that all kinds of communities could accept as their own.

The Jeffersonian image pictured identical local, state, and national hierarchies linked one to another by their leaders. Only the scope of responsibilities distinguished one unit from the next—microcosm from macrocosm—and only the intrusion of a diabolical elite disturbed the normal harmony among them. Barring interference, the system naturally elevated men according to their merit and breeding, just as at its lower levels it freed men's reason to recognize and validate good policy. Excellent local leaders rose to guide their states, and outstanding ones their nation; average citizens from time to time set aside their private affairs to listen and judge. Vague in its specification of duties, benign in its acceptance of a diffusion of power, it, like Hamilton's scheme, left broad realms of national policy to a leader's initiative, while it covered ordinary social relations in a haze of voluntarism and mutualism that eminently suited a nation of insular, suspicious parts. Although slaves and the urban poor held ambiguous places in the system, it was a remarkably inclusive one for the eighteenth century. If Hamilton was the centralist, the Jeffersonians were truly the nationalists. Not only did their vision triumph after the 1790s, but even most Federalists hastily adapted to its general outlines. Never again would a major public figure openly challenge the ideal of an American wholeness.

For the Jeffersonians, like all eighteenth-century leaders, the ultimate test was not how well their vision suited the nation but how well America fit their system. Their arrangement of graded and interlinked social relationships, as they understood it, was intrinsically, not empirically true. Principles first, then behavior. Among its important implications was a resistance to rapid personal mobility. Its tiers acted in this sense as barriers—certainly not impassable yet always formidable—ensuring a deliberate pace of mobility either upward or downward. With opportunities spread like a feast before them early in the nineteenth century, Americans discarded these restraints. They had been difficult enough to maintain in the late eighteenth century when the Revolution in particular had shuffled places and fortunes; after all, the new nation had lifted Hamilton, born a bastard, to the peak of power. By the nineteenth century all the traditional barriers had become a legacy of traps, as the chances for advancement were enticing not only the well-to-do but people throughout the old hierarchies. A set of pre-existing dividers, once blurred, was now erased.

With that crucial change came a new vision. The tiers of the eighteenth century became the staircase of the nineteenth, with the hope of mounting and the fear of falling central to its meaning. In contrast to eighteenth-century America, the new society appeared at times even more like an elevator shaft than a stairway. Nothing, it was assumed, would slow the pace other than intrinsic qualities of character, and such popular images as the happy rise from log cabin to President and the implacable descent of anyone who dared taste alcohol sharpened that message. These measures of character also sorted members of a community. Rather than achieving levels, people battled for advantage in a kinetic, expansive society of uncertain criteria. What Florence Kluckholn has noted as a characteristic of modern western culture—the need in all social relationships to establish dominance and subordinance —operated with a special force in communities that no longer had a chart of stations to guide them. Each compartment required an extraordinary variety of contests to help locate members in a world of flux. Swapping and betting, pitting one farm against another and testing this against that scheme for railroad development, competitions of every dimension by makeshift rules, accompanied the perpetual drive to grow or die, to succeed by standards that were now inevitably relative.

Problems of community cohesion in the nineteenth century were inherently no more severe than they had been in the eighteenth. Constant interaction could give the new communities an impressive element of popular participation, a sense of common involvement that rallied all kinds of people in behalf of development and defense. During the 1830s, rich and poor in Cincinnati attended mass meetings to consider new ventures in transportation just as they joined mobs to eradicate abolitionism. The nineteenth-century community invited citizens to assume responsibilities that in the eighteenth had belonged automatically to those at the top, and the preservation of a community's unity now relied upon those who would take it as their task, usually families of higher than average success who checked immorality and arrogance above them and policed dissipation and misbehavior below them. The middle of the compartment, therefore, served generally as its critical point of maintenance, the center of memory about good and bad families, of judgments about frugality and decency, and of those gradual alterations in local values that were essential to a community's cohesion.

As in the case of the Jeffersonian vision, what applied to individuals and families inside a community held equally for communities inside a state, or states and regions inside a nation. Each larger realm reenacted life along the stairway, with units rising and falling according to their merit—their character, as the personifications of the nineteenth century explained it. Once again, virtue and reward were assumed to coincide; once again, the sorting process was expected to distribute the units in such a way that all would still find places within a common whole. It was a system predicated upon ignorance and isolation, upon bits of information, weak communication, and a large measure of indifference. Bursts of news and struggles for dear resources almost always distorted the image. The more Southerners heard and cared about Northerners in the antebellum years, the more pernicious an equation between their morality and economic success became. Later in the century industrial and financial magnates, by means very few communities acknowledged as legitimate, were piling huge fortunes that separated them from the rest of society and were then used—so the popular tales went—for devious and corrupt purposes. Railroads, once seen vaguely as the facilitator of everyone's enterprise, emerged as giants in their own right, exacting tribute from each town along their routes. Too great an awareness of trusts and immigrant hordes and the debaucheries of city life eventually destroyed the illusion of a national system that operated by the logic of a community.

What had disappeared by the end of the nineteenth century was the sense of leeway, of those expansive opportunities essential to a society of geographically separated units in parallel enterprise. Now the nation seemed filled. Signals of progress in an earlier time had become omens of disaster. Cities appeared huge and choked, corporations omnipresent and overpowering. Businessmen large and small complained of a new, unmanageable competition. Immigrants, once fresh labor in a land of promise, swarmed and smothered native Americans. And the frontier, it was announced, had closed. Where could people go? A frightening sense of entanglement and impingement forced Americans to recalculate the basis for their society and therefore the meaning of America's wholeness.

Some stubbornly refused to abandon the traditional standards. If a multitude of small enterprises established a healthy economy, then smash the trusts and enforce the old competition. If ethnic homogeneity defined the community, then stop immigration and Americanize those who were here. If liquor was an evil at home, then ban it everywhere. At times of confidence, nineteenth-century Americans had been able to assume that the people who mattered were already abiding by the values of the community. Now the evidence of diversity was too overwhelming to ignore, and a national society that could not be avoided would have to be purified.

The new occupational elite devised a very different answer. Starting with the functions that people performed instead of the places they lived, this solution welcomed and then regulated the growing mass of interconnections. Initially through such agglomerates as business, finance, agriculture, and labor, later through more and more specialized economic and professional segments, it pictured the nation as a set of angled planes touching and intersecting each other in complex patterns that ultimately coordinated in a single system. Each unit—furniture manufacturers, linotype operators, contract lawyers, chemical engineers—had a distinct identity and function; the vitality of each, in turn, relied upon the vitality of the whole. Unlike previous images of unity that had appeared the same from all sides, this one required three dimensions to express its complicated network of linkages and interactions.

For the first time since Hamilton's evanescent dream, a vision of the whole nation contained a rationale of its own, a meaning greater than that of a segment writ large. It was a truly national system, with rules and rewards that gave primacy to a national political economy: the autonomy of its major functional units, a supportive government facilitating their interaction, a citizenry geared to production and consumption in a disciplined free market, and everyone mutually dependent on the system's smooth operation. Nineteenth-century society had allowed considerable speculation on monetary policies or taxation or a soft socialism in industrial relations. Political economy, like the weather, demanded attention but defied local control. Debate here had been an honorable avocation, just as it had been intolerable on those matters of sex and family and religion that did underwrite the community. A twentieth-century elite, increasingly the nationwide audience for explorations into moral relativism, now met heterodox economic and political theories with a quick, hard response. A vigorous antiradicalism in public and a liberal private library were no more paradoxical in the twentieth century than a pinched provincialism in morals and a receptivity to the impulsive economic plunge had been in the nineteenth. In place of nineteenth-century education in citizenship, which had emphasized such values as thrift, sobriety, and cleanliness, the modern elite version was organized around a catechism on civics and the marketplace. The devil of the nineteenth century had been a gambling, drinking profligate; in the twentieth, he was a leveling, regimenting communist. Something called American Capitalism had now joined the holy order of liberty and opportunity, often as a shorthand expression for both of them.

A national system implied some degree of acceptance everywhere in order to function. The boundaries of the United States acquired a new importance as the necessary container for all loyalties, and no feelings stronger than nostalgia were

expected to spill beyond its borders. Such concepts as hyphen-
ism and socialism, connoting a divided or an international allegiance, roused not just scorn but an immediate concern.
Such slogans as My Country Right or Wrong, America Love
It or Leave It, expressed, among other things, a powerful elite
need. In the nineteenth century, cultural deviants reviewed
from afar could be acknowledged and then excluded from the
true America; in the twentieth, ideological deviants viewed
from the top had to be converted or removed. That perception,
which was already a significant element in the Red Scare after
the First World War, developed into the dominant theme of
McCarthyism after the Second World War.

Tasks in the national system were increasingly mandatory.
Voluntarism, which in the nineteenth century had meant the
freedom of doing or not doing, lost its optional quality in the
twentieth and came instead to describe a private rather than
a government management of the system's responsibilities. In
a system of functions, everyone had to have a role and with it
an appropriate category. An elite simply projected the logic
of their lives into an entire society. The farther downward
they peered, the dimmer their vision became and the more
creativity it entailed. Artificial units such as assembly-line operators and department-store clerks and tenant farmers told
far more about the demands of the system for completeness
than it did about the way these people actually defined their
own lives. Yet no matter how often people in such imaginary
groups acted from a very different base of values, an elite still
found a standardized box for the evidence: new data on the
attitudes of factory workers, not data requiring new categories.

From the bottom of the national system, Americans had far
less difficulty recognizing the great distance between an elite's
life and their own. Even the connecting paths were obscure.
In its early years the new system had retained some prospects
of the nineteenth-century's open, simple climb upward. The
worship of Henry Ford, a country boy whose everyday in-

genuity had apparently propelled him to the top, and the popular accounts in the late 1920s of turning elementary shrewdness on the stock market into limitless wealth had kept a portion of the old dream alive. It had not been unreasonable to believe, as Willy Loman told his boys in *Death of a Salesman,* that a knack and a style could still achieve wonders. But as most Americans recognized by the 1940s, it was Bernard, the studious boy next door, not Biff Loman, who had found the passage. A shift from life adjustment to skills in the public schools, an intense concern for achievement scores, and a rush to the universities expressed an understanding that mobility in a sophisticated scheme of functions required peculiar kinds of knowledge, knowledge so abstruse at the upper levels that a vaulting leap for an adult was almost certainly mere fantasy. The professions in particular presented an array of specialized sanctuaries, each with its own idiom and procedure, where even the qualifications for entry could not be explained in ordinary language. As if all families toward the bottom had become nineteenth-century immigrants, parents could only lament their own lack of training and invest hopes in their children.

Qualitative differences in values throughout American society intensified the urge to coerce. The cultural wholeness still critical to the security of many who operated at the lower levels of the national system seemed unobtainable on any other terms. The failure of so many Americans to abide by the logic of the new system struck members of the elite as a blend of the perverse and the sinister. If people were too backward, too stupid to understand the self-evident needs of their world, they should be forced to behave intelligently. Willful resistance was a kind of subversion. How else interpret striking miners in wartime, the reelection of brazenly corrupt officials, the impossible demands for service placed on doctors or lawyers or corporations? In the decentralized society of the nineteenth century, isolation could soften the implications of such differences. In a compact society where interdependence was unavoidable, these persistent problems of national cohesion had a disturbingly refractory cast.

To agree on a need for coercion but to disagree on the substance of unity exposed the very differences that Americans were striving to overcome. The calls for cultural uniformity that regularly attracted a wide following had no natural relationship with the ideological conformity that engaged elites, and through confusions of this sort such a broadly popular impulse as McCarthyism eventually fragmented into mutually suspicious pieces. Only the radical youth of the 1960s managed to violate so many canons of national cohesion that almost everyone else could at least agree upon ostracizing them. One consequence of these continuing frustrations was a multiplication of the number and frequency of symbols declaring a whole society: displays of the American flag and strains of the national anthem, concern for such common duties as voting and conscription, tokens of a common citizenship such as the ethnically mixed classroom and the interracial handshake. Yet not even these symbols could escape the ambiguities of segmented wholeness. For some the American flag expressed a new integrated nationalism; for others it represented just one more circle of protection around a cultural enclave, a meaning they revealed by the easy interchangeability of American and Confederate flags as equally appropriate symbols of allegiance.

An even more refined set of differences was exposed by disagreements over a scale of prestige for the national society. Toward the top of the modern system, claims and counterclaims measured public against private success, businesses against professions, subspecialty against subspecialty in a tangle of contests that had no resolution. Toward the bottom, the simultaneous attraction of a distant elite ladder and need for a standard more suitable to daily life gave everybody's homemade design its own validity. The common denominator was diversity. Polls in 1970 and 1971 that selected Billy Graham, Spiro Agnew, Pope Paul VI, Ralph Nader, and Bob Hope among the men Americans most admired may have indicated something about the weakness of professional values and the strength of mass publicity, but they could help no one frame a national scheme of prestige. Precisely such substitutes as polls came to have exceptional utility as a guide to the blind, a spontaneous, democratic authority that could give coherence to a confusing world. An attention to the details of winning and losing that had once concentrated locally was now turned across the nation. Lists of books and movies and recipes and candidates—everything's top ten—expressed a general impulse to rank the otherwise scattered bits of modern society.

By far the most powerful cement of the new system was consumption. Gradually and rather vaguely, Americans had first shown an awareness of themselves specifically as consumers in the two decades before the First World War. This consciousness touched a variety of local reforms, as David Thelen has indicated, and infused such national issues as the tariff and antitrust with new arguments about retail prices and standards of living. The war itself, through nationwide publicity on incomes, prices, and purchases, accelerated that trend into the 1920s when mass consumption became one foundation of the developing national system. The role of the consumer, once established, steadily expanded: the beneficiary in the 1920s, the pump-primer in the 1930s, the disciplined soldier of the home front in the 1940s, the passionate object of courtship in the 1950s, the equivalent of citizen by the 1960s. As consumption changed from a privilege to a duty, the system accommodated in response. Consumption, everybody's stake in society, offered a ready ideological answer to everything from class cleavage to civil rights. Where else but America provided such an abundance of goods and services? Consumer credit became a critical national resource. Business competition acquired a new meaning in the cause of greater mass consumption, and against grim resistance businessmen lost some of their autonomy in pricing and distribution. Retailing in certain lower-priced items at last began to verify the graphs of the classical economists.

Popular response outstripped every accommodation. Successful Americans had long found goods and services a useful means of displaying their worth. Now the less successful discovered in consumption an indispensable compensation for the aridity of their jobs. As David Bazelon has noted, the crucial importance of regular employment was the credit it generated: to countless Americans the meaning of work had become the power to spend. A flow of income, credit, and purchase supplied the rationale for innumerable marriages, and women as primary consumers enjoyed what was for them an unprecedented range of authority. Rather than either a privilege or a duty, consumption had developed into an inalienable right. It was the most enticing carrot dangled before GI's during the Second World War; it was central to the crusade against Communism, which, according to the standard tales, would take away those precious cars and houses. By the 1960s, when urban blacks in the midst of riot helped themselves to the goods a society had promised but denied them, almost all Americans, one way or another, had stated this cardinal principle of their social contract. Thus when Ralph Nader championed the self-evident right of Americans to sound, inexpensive products, millions received him as their tribune. Clearly consumption had been the wild horse of the new ideology, forever beyond its leaders' control. Yet nothing less than this kind of driving, popular passion could have generated a sense of wholeness in modern America.

From the Jeffersonian republic to the consumer society, the need to see a whole America reflecting the dominant qualities of the segment created the primary stress within each formulation of national unity. And in each century it was a combination of ignorance and restraint—sometimes calculated, usually circumstantial—that held these tensions to a tolerable level. Only the abstractness of republican ideology and the looseness of eighteenth-century social connections preserved a delicate thread between the deistic founding fathers and Pennsylvania Germans. A sense of distant cities, distant competitors, distant immigrants, and an extraordinary faith in the capacity of communities to harness a canal or a railroad to their local purposes protected nineteenth-century society from the consequences of its diversity and enterprise. Even the inability to maintain an illusion of parallelism between North and South did not stop Americans after the Civil War from constructing another version of the same system.

For an occupational elite, the ideal relationship between segment and nation changed in the twentieth century; now they expected a nation of units to operate *like* they did, not live *as* they did. But ignorance and restraint were no less crucial. An elite simply could not afford to believe, for example, that the agreement in the 1960s between Klansmen and black radicals on the desirability of a separate nation for America's blacks actually expressed a widespread sentiment. It was equally fundamental to deemphasize cultural or moral issues in national policy. Around mid-century the greatest threat to a popular faith in American cohesion was the move to nationalize standards in such areas as race relations, religion in schools, and local law enforcement, and Richard Nixon's greatest service to an elite system was his leadership in decentralizing those controls. A tenuous American unity had always required the right to a safe place for those who fell somewhere inside the real America but could not affect it—Connecticut Baptists in the late eighteenth century, respectable communitarians in the nineteenth, white Alabama farmers in the twentieth.

Nothing in the nature of these many visions prescribed the distance between top and bottom. Century by century each variation required a sense of wholeness without the specifications to measure it, a steady popular faith in cohesion without the means to verify it. The challenge of maintaining an acceptable yet indeterminate distance among the elements of American society was one more index to the stress inherent in the search for unity.

The Jeffersonian scheme was born in a revolutionary era deeply concerned about the excesses of elite privilege and the civic implications of poverty and ignorance; and part of its genius was a fine sensitivity to these anxieties. The ostentatious frugality of Republican administrations and the rhetoric of what James Sterling Young has called antipower values helped to shrink the apparent distance between government and citizen, even if they did not significantly curb the prerogatives of leadership. Jeffersonian antiurbanism expressed, above all, a rural society's uneasiness about the city rabble, and it identified virtuous poverty as agrarian and dispersed. Precisely in the areas of Jeffersonian strength Hamilton's system aggravated these American fears: the bold acceptance of elite privilege and the inevitability of controls over an undependable poor. Even as self-conscious an elitist as John Adams, who would have set apart the office of President through titles and ceremony, limited the risks of his Federalism by a personal austerity and a public dedication to the cohesive town meeting. In the first several decades after the Revolution, the rights of citizenship in many states were gradually extended to a larger proportion of the poor, and leaders almost everywhere were increasingly expected to acknowledge citizen sovereignty. Federalists as well as Republicans, finding it less and less expedient to await a call for office, learned to greet the voters and debate their views.

What had strained against the eighteenth-century hierarchy exploded in the expansive world of the nineteenth. Without the mediation of a social scale that justified at least certain differences, the task of containing top and bottom lost a stable point of reference. Now it was relative wealth more than any other standard that set the terms of the challenge. Although corporate privilege and family pretensions had their opponents, the greatest attention concentrated on "those extremes of opulence and penury, each of which unhumanizes the mind." In a mobile, adventurous age, few could know in detail how neighbors had acquired their wealth or even how much of it they had. The primary test here as elsewhere in the nineteenth century became use, or public behavior. The cardinal sin of the rich, as Dr. Walter Channing of Boston stated in 1843, was "Exclusiveness." "By our modes of life—our houses—our dress—our equipage; in short by what is strictly external to us . . . men detach themselves from their neighbors—withdraw themselves from the human family. . . ." An acceptance of egalitarian values and a concern for community affairs could secure a place inside the bounds of unity for almost all fortunes, but wealthy citizens were still watched with a keener eye, judged by a closer standard, than middling families. The urge to uplift the poor expressed fundamentally a social need, and its rhetoric coupled the attacks on moral weakness with guarantees of readily available opportunity to demonstrate that individual failures, not social flaws, depressed the bottom of society. Even then, the poor could never be ignored, only exhorted again and again to emulate the behavior of their betters.

To control the implications of wealth in this fashion required a sense of open channels, so that everybody could be reminded of the values applicable to all. Late in the nineteenth century, as information about the nation's rich and poor was spreading rapidly, these avenues of communication seemed to close. Great new fortunes were encased in impenetrable corporate structures and exclusive patterns of private life. If, as Rockefeller said in appropriate nineteenth-century humility, God had given him his money, He had certainly not bestowed trusts and banking syndicates in the bargain.

Grandiose philanthropies—acres of public park, whole symphony orchestras—might demonstrate something akin to community involvement, but the world of Newport and the Four Hundred told only of a haughty removal from the rest of society. The rich, it appeared, were buying personal exemptions from American morality. A mass of urban laborers, dressing and speaking and worshiping in bewildering varieties of strangeness, generated the same feeling of channels blocked. Quantity and quality—the size of the challenge and its nature —merged in a sense of helplessness. Who could even reach the corporate nabob or the immigrant poor? Until the end of the century, Americans offered basically moral solutions to this crisis of unity, for as they understood it social morality was the crux of the issue. But what they called the Social Question—the consequences of concentrated wealth and concentrated poverty—exceeded their capacities to manage.

By the twentieth century most communities had become simply residential areas, with scarcely any powers of sanction. Italian-Americans in Chicago might remember Al Capone warmly for passing money among the neighborhood children, townspeople might honor a distant and successful son for the bequest of a public swimming pool, but they could no longer even tacitly require these responses. They merely received in gratitude. Only the most outrageous sources of wealth damaged a family's standing in the suburbs. Even zoning ordinances, which attempted to exclude the people whom neighbors would no longer try to reach, seldom withstood the ambitions of realtors, and the poor continued to filter into all except the most exclusive corners of the metropolis.

The occupational units of the twentieth century compensated with some rules of containment. Relatively weak groups, such as public school teachers and industrial unions, relied on a closely graded scale of pay and privileges as their protection against an undue spread among members. The executive level of the large corporations used a similar, although much more grandly constructed ladder of rewards, both as an incentive and as an integrator. Prosperous professions that could reasonably assure an expanding plenty for everyone inside the segment employed far looser controls. Beginners who provided routine services for meager pay—recruits to the law factories, medical interns, research and teaching assistants in graduate school—were defined as transients and informed that after an apprenticeship they too would enjoy the full advantages of their professions. At the top, prominent lawyers or doctors who did not dissemble involvement in the ordinary affairs of the bar or the hospital, preeminent academicians who neither taught nor attended to university matters, felt at least some counter-pull of disapproval from their colleagues.

None of these new techniques held much promise in creating the impression of a whole society. To preserve an American unity against the strains of wealth and poverty in the twentieth century increasingly required some form of national regulation. If an impersonal national system determined the distribution of rewards, then this same kind of system would have to supervise the consequences. Nothing symbolized the shift more clearly than the federal income tax, a nationwide bureaucratic replacement for community controls that by the 1940s had become an indispensable agent in the cause of American cohesion. The purpose of the income tax was to contain the upper levels of the national system. Beginning in the 1930s, various legislative provisions for social security comprised its base. Like the tax laws, social security communicated an ideal. What holes it left in the floor, how stingy its support in a rich land, did not necessarily alter the appearance of a national unity nationally sustained.

A national unity that was predicated on the distribution of wealth demanded that the entire society seem to rise and fall together. In prosperous times, more and more people each decade used a widening range of public information to check their progress against competitive groups or favored occupa-

tions or national averages. In the abbreviated forms of the
news releases, wage scales, inflation rates, and cost-of-living
indices not only enjoyed a broad popular audience but generated fierce debates over equity, debates that invariably relied upon somebody else's relative advantage in the system
for their justification. Depression aggravated these already
intense concerns. No more devastating revelations followed
the crash of 1929 than the stories of how certain financial and
corporate leaders had extracted personal profits from their
collapsing companies. Images of the distraught banker leap-
ing from a skyscraper window and the ruined businessman in
his frayed silk hat selling apples on the corner carried a significant social message in the midst of suffering and insecu-
rity. Later, when William Benton and Chester Bowles became prominent liberal Democrats, they buried as deep from
view as they could the millions they had made through advertising during the Great Depression. Nixon's freeze on wages
in 1971 satisfied this sense of uniform hardship with an impressive simplicity. Whatever elementary logic and ample
evidence said to the contrary, it created an essential illusion
of equalized deprivation, and in a ratio of 6 to 1, Americans
told the polltakers they approved.

An otherwise impersonal national system required a pro-
fusion of signs from the mighty that they remained a part of
the whole. Leaders in national government, increasingly removed and powerful, regularly left their offices to mix with
citizens and carefully publicized their endearing habits and
family attachments. Corporations made rule by the stockhold-
ers a fetish, complete with annual meetings and solemn elections and photographs of ordinary folk mingling with the officers, not because many people would believe in an actual
business democracy but because the ritual itself bespoke a
commitment to the right values. The occasional, widely heralded conviction of an important businessman or politician
reinforced a faith in democratic justice protecting the nation

from excessive privilege. In a consumer society the use of common goods and services became a social obligation. If the newsboy could no longer dream of the Presidency, he could still walk in the same shoes to the same ballpark and eat the same hot dog as the candidate courting his parents' vote. Eventually this same logic required the removal of formal barriers against a particular religion or skin color or sex: all must have access to the national system, whatever might then happen to them inside. To picture the poorest and richest differing only in degree, not in kind, meant that an American unity was still intact.

The most horrible vision of a shattered society was one of class cleavage—Hamilton's crucial weakness, Europe's ominous example, industrialism's standing danger. American hypersensitivity to any hint of a broad union across the top or bottom of society revealed itself during the first years of the republic in the vicious cries against Monocrats and Jacobins. By the nineteenth century something explicitly called class had materialized as the primary enemy. From attacks on a dead but symbolically portentous Federalism early in the century through assaults on corporate aristocrats to accusations of a military-industrial complex, the possibility of a privileged class, rather than merely privileged people, provided the standard climax to charges of tyranny from above. Prospects of an unusually successful appeal to poor and unorganized Americans immediately brought screams of demagogue: one who employed novel cues (labeled emotional tricks) rallying citizens to unorthodox ends (labeled class hatred). Men as different as Andrew Jackson and Thaddeus Stevens, William Jennings Bryan and Samuel Gompers, Franklin Roosevelt and Huey Long aroused a special animus on just these grounds of mobilizing a class below.

In each century, the images of wholeness were specifically designed to counter any possibility of class. As Gordon Wood has shown, patrician concern in the 1780s over the connecting strands and independent initiatives among common citizens contributed substantially to the drive for a new, stabilizing Constitution, and soon after it was adopted, widespread anxieties over a Federalist ruling elite underwrote Republican victory. The Jeffersonian scheme responded to both dangers. Its links from national to state to local levels ran from leader to leader; ordinary citizens would await the word flowing down that channel, not across the society from other ordinary citizens. Natural human ties would also pull the nation's elite back to their localities, thereby preserving society's roots in its communities. The lines of attachment, in other words, were always vertical, never horizontal. The vertical lines of the nineteenth century represented the yardsticks of success, the means by which each unit—individual, family, community— measured its place within an open society of merit rewarded. In the flux of units rising and falling, permanent lateral connections, it was said, would only force the unwary to the lowest common denominator of the class, where the vices of the weakest would sink their stronger companions. Alliances of convenience, yes; but these must always be selective and transient, never broad and lasting. The multiplicity of intersecting planes in the twentieth-century system offered paths of mobility within each occupation and certain causeways from one occupation to another, a complex of stairs and cables and crossings now inviting a leap upward, now slowing movement to a crawl. The intricacy of the passage, the extreme difficulty of calculating unusual routes, meant that a hazardous step sideways risked everything. The consequence of a class experiment was no legitimate perch anywhere on the scaffolding.

Transitions from one social system to another generated the most acute stress over class. As faith in a customary scheme of unity disappeared, the specter of class spread irresistibly in its wake. Appropriate to an expanding, decentralized nation, the scramble at the beginning of the nineteenth century to protect an unguarded America was noisy and often chaotic.

Nevertheless, it accumulated an impressive record. As defenses against an upper class, Americans in many states removed the exclusive rules of entry into such professions as the law and the ministry, resisted the proposals to incorporate new business enterprises, and opened public offices to more and more people of average standing. As protections against a working class, others established common schools in the cities, organized an array of Protestant missions to discipline the poor, and labored to contain the Catholic church. By the 1840s the maturing of nineteenth-century society had allayed the sharpest of these anxieties.

The class crisis of the late nineteenth and the early twentieth century was both more pervasive and more prolonged. The nineteenth-century vision of wholeness had concentrated Americans at the middle level of society, where units competed to differentiate themselves from others of modest success. A rapid industrial growth late in the century seemed to squeeze that bulging middle as it forced millions to the bottom and elevated a few to the top. Although neither image could have withstood a hard statistical test, the one still communicated social strength, as nineteenth-century Americans understood it, and the other an imminent social disaster. The most prominent critics late in the century, such as Henry George, Henry Demarest Lloyd, and the Populists, demanded only that society be allowed to return to its natural form. Even as their warnings grew more frantic and their predictions more catastrophic, they refused to use class as an answer to class. Whatever the trials of the present, the future would have to dissolve all broad divisions in a homogeneous and prosperous unity.

It was an economic elite who departed from the sacred American standard by accepting class conflict. Obsessed by the horror of a European working class arriving with industrialism, they marshaled political power, legal precedents, and armed forces late in the century on the assumption that class had come to stay. While an increasing diversity in ethnic groups, laboring skills, and agricultural economics was fragmenting the lower level of society, an elite not only clung to their cause; they even made progress in creating an upper class out of the illusion of a lower class. Perhaps nothing so limited their powers over public policy early in the twentieth century as their stubborn fantasy of a permanent, self-conscious laboring class in a nation that could not long tolerate this particular form of hysteria.

The failure to manage problems of class according to its traditional values was crippling to nineteenth-century society, and that weakness preoccupied Americans as they rebuilt early in the twentieth. One answer with a sturdy nineteenth-century heritage was the destruction of labor organizations wherever they appeared, an approach publicized by the National Association of Manufacturers and adopted by a host of employers and their sympathizers from Lawrence to Los Angeles. In the crusade against socialism during and just after the First World War, a version of this answer momentarily became national policy. A second and equally traditional approach attracted its major support from townspeople and farmers who could not hope to compete on economic terms with an urban-industrial system and who demanded instead a culturally uniform nation as a solution to all class differences. Through prohibition and immigration restriction, their answer also won notable victories, and through the KKK and the fundamentalist crusade it revealed a large though poorly integrated constituency.

The solution that eventually dominated national policy discarded the relatively simple conceptions of uniformity from the nineteenth-century tradition. It met the challenge of class division not by attempting to erase the lines of difference but by multiplying them. Appealing in particular to the most successful farmers and wage-earners, it promised an increasing flow of rewards to those who would organize and identify their interests according to the narrowest possible occupational category. At the same time, this solution required an acceptance of occupational segmentation as a system, one in which all units would abide by the same rules of procedure, recognize their interdependence, and acknowledge an elite's leadership over general economic policy. In contrast to the preoccupations of the nineteenth century, classless now expressed an evil equivalent to class: the removal of all socioeconomic barriers was just as threatening as the erection of the wrong ones. It was an exceptionally effective answer. Not only did farming and laboring segments proliferate; their spokesmen proved very responsive to elite economic leadership and very quick to cry the terrors of communism or socialism.

What the elite solution ignored was the other half of the problem that had overwhelmed nineteenth-century society, a class above. To meet this danger Americans looked to the national government, which was expected to act as the impartial agent of the public interest. In particular, an expanding range of regulatory laws with bureaus and commissions to implement them were charged to guard the nation against a privileged corporate class. Although this system of defense never quite lost all plausibility, it brought at least as much frustration as comfort. First, it relied upon an obsolete democratic model of citizens assigning public officials to watch special interests, then watching the officials to keep them honest. In the labyrinthine processes of a modern political economy, the complexity of regulation so vastly exceeded an ordinary citizen's capacity to understand that only experts could debate with other experts over its technical operations. Most Americans turned instead to someone else—anyone else—who would take the time and acquire the skills to do their watching for them. Second, this same apparatus was expected to eliminate any friction among business groups that might interfere with the system's smooth functioning. As an economic mechanism, it required an intimate cooperation between a corporate elite and the national government; as social protection, it demanded a clear line between the two. No magic formula could resolve the contradiction. Fears of an upper class, therefore, remained endemic to a society that had only its passion for economic growth to ease the anxieties over corporate power.

The major social transitions early in the nineteenth and early in the twentieth century coincided with the two most complicated and concentrated periods of reform in American history. Both released powerful feelings of liberation from an inhibiting past and great expectations for a dawning new era. They expressed, in one sense, the high energy that came from emancipation, the unique excitement that accompanied a sudden revelation of promise with seemingly limitless means for realizing it. Exploring the possibilities of a new society was a heady experience. At the same time, each brought as a solemn obligation the reunification of a society that actually was splintering. Attacks against class were just one element in the general cause of cohesion. Reformers drew upon the past for goals as they experimented with new ways of reaching them; they sought to legitimize authority as they probed the boundaries of a new freedom. Because unity was a perennial puzzle, because America's wholeness could never really be assumed, liberalism in its most intensely flourishing states always included a special containing urge. To rephrase Louis Hartz, the fulfillment of John Locke's liberalism in America required a dedication to Edmund Burke's cohesion.

In a society struggling to define itself, the tension between release and control always generated anxieties, and a time of upheaval greatly intensified them. Every process associated with reform—the Great Awakening, the Revolution, Reconstruction, the New Deal, the New Frontier–Great Society programs—was swept by these emotions, and in their various plans, the reformers themselves would never have been able to disentangle the elements of freedom and restraint. It made no sense to try. In the early temperance movement, the Freedman's Bureau, the Federal Trade Commission, the National Labor Relations Board, and the civil rights laws, among innumerable examples, an expansion of opportunities and a tightening of discipline both belonged to a single purpose.

What each clustering of reforms sought to achieve was a new social integration, a higher form of social harmony. That longing for cohesion flowed at the heart of the Great Awakening, the revolutionary era, the new nationalism of early Reconstruction, and the new wholeness that Franklin Roosevelt and Lyndon Johnson envisaged. The successful reform movement demanded—perhaps only for a brief time—a powerful sense of gathering forces, of people everywhere awakening, listening, moving. If in retrospect the parts of the movement seemed hopelessly dispersed and often at odds, the contemporary illusion of a people on the march in a swelling army gave the process its essential justification, unity through change. Expose the differences, confront the contradictions, dispel the illusion, and the movement dissolved. The regularity with which these movements were followed so quickly by periods of conservative strength—the late 1780s and 1790s, the 1870s, the 1920s, the 1940s, the late 1960s and early 1970s—represented neither a mystical rhythm, a pull toward equilibrium, nor necessarily a calculated counterattack. It required merely a minor adjustment in the tension between release and control to produce that kind of shift. If reform did not bring a faith in unity, something else must. Yesterday's reformers could reverse tactics with absolute consistency, for in America a sense of wholeness was an end that dictated its means. A segmented society could not function without it.

# ~V~

## *The Politics of the Social Contract*

"POLITICS," BERNARD CRICK HAS WRITTEN, "is a way of ruling divided societies without undue violence. . . ." A segmented society with its special aversion to disorder charged politics with a particularly broad and basic range of responsibilities, a set of commandments to preserve liberty within the compartments while maintaining a common society among them. In America political inventiveness was not merely a national talent; it was a national necessity.

From early colonial times the requirements of politics were fixed by the primacy of local affairs. The particularism of many self-centered units—families, congregations, towns, counties—gave politics at any more removed level a discontinuous quality, a pull always back to the specific, limited concerns of these compartments. Collecting an appreciable number of units into an alliance was extremely difficult, for their narrow involvements surrounded each segment in an atmosphere of indifference to other ambitions and mistrust of other motives. Feelings of gratitude or loyalty, especially toward a distant power, rarely accumulated; they, like the objectives of politics, were almost always matters isolated in time and place, the consequence of small bargains made, fulfilled, and forgotten. People from abroad whose sense of politics was a network of interdependence and reciprocity found the colonies incomprehensible. William Penn, for example, along with countless agents of royal government, never grasped the thin, formalistic meaning of allegiance among the colonists and learned only in desperation to calculate policy on the assumption that the reservoir of credit and general good will would almost certainly be dry.

From the perspective of a provincial capital or London, colonial politics acquired a predictable rhythm of assertion and resistance. Instructions that assumed the prerogative of rulers and the responsibility of subjects—a permanent, predefined relationship both natural and legal—came to most of the colonial segments either as irrelevancies or as intrusions, and the more their governors insisted, the more they were likely to resist. The imperatives of war strained the ability of colonial governments to act at all; the prolonged crisis in imperial relations after 1763 eventually smashed the entire system. It was in this realm of challenge and response that patterns of mutual interest formed, that compartments or their representatives not only leagued together in defense against a distant, aggrandizing power but even accumulated the results of these contests into protective traditions—the liberties of a town, the rights of a lower house in the legislature. Colonial politics in the eighteenth century showed such a negative cast not because the colonists lacked positive objectives but because only the defensive ones had the continuity to define general procedures and goals.

British policy in the 1760s and 1770s managed to communicate such an array of threats to so many colonial segments that they extended their protective traditions into revolution. Once activated, this identification of politics with the most basic liberties did not easily die, and a form of total politics continued to reappear during the early years of the republic, especially in the 1790s. This style of politics by its nature tended to elevate issues into principles, to distill differences into abstract truths, and the hierarchical structure of late eighteenth-century America enabled leaders, from time to time, to mobilize a diversity of segments for a specific crisis, much as an army might be mustered for a grand display of unity, then dispersed. Total politics, defending a whole way of life, clearly suggested the analogue of war. Because it aggravated conflicts as it expressed them, it generated a stress that, if sustained for a considerable period, would surely have destroyed the new nation.

Yet even in the era of the founding fathers, total politics was in many respects unnatural, a response to extraordinary tensions across a society that remained fundamentally a collection of small spheres and local involvements. A keen sense of the colonial legacy and a strong desire to read the inevitable as desirable made Madison's *Federalist Number Ten* a fitting statement to launch the republican experiment: space and diversity, the shrewd Virginian declared, would be the guarantors of liberty in a dispersed and heterogeneous nation. The increasing difficulty of calling forth tableaux of partisan strength during the troubled years between 1807 and 1814 indicated how many of America's units were irretrievably lost to their particular interests and would never again react to the old cues. By 1815 the facade of total politics had disintegrated, and the scramble of the nineteenth century had begun.

In one sense politics in the nineteenth century represented a far larger and noisier version of colonial practices. Segments seeking specific benefits found the eighteenth-century tradition of narrowly contractual politics—of bargain and run— very well suited to their innumerable schemes for development, and qualities of interdependence and reciprocation remained almost as alien as they had been before the Revolution. Strong feelings of mutuality thrived only in crises of protection, then dissipated in conflicts over economic advantage. In other important ways, however, the pattern of politics altered radically. The growth that communities so avidly sought carried their attention outward along lines of transportation and commerce that connected their interests with a wider world. Towns, counties, states, territories acquired a new geographical concreteness, and nineteenth-century Americans, quite literally mapping their plans, expanded their areas of political relevance according to the geography of their ambitions. Beginning early in the century, an extraordinary array of these enterprises for development demanded assistance from state governments. Later, some grand schemes in commerce and manufacture pushed onward to the national government, and the grandest, associated especially with the major houses of finance, even lost their ties to any geographical base. But throughout the century there were far more losers contracting or remapping their realms than there were winners extending theirs. Rapid shifts in argument from local to state to national rights and back again followed the logic of a system where the only tests of consistency were the immediate requirements of everybody's specific ambitions.

At any time in the nineteenth century, therefore, politics expressed a multitude of plans and demands overlapping one another, each calculated to serve a particular interest, each competing for attention in one or more jurisdictions, each indifferent or hostile to the others. Local politicians represented these interests much as lawyers did their clients and received rewards according to the hopes and benefits they could bring home. The importance of fitting these many ambitions into their appropriate jurisdictions forced most politicians to specialize at just one level of government. If they changed levels, they not only needed another assortment of skills and connections, but they also had to abandon most of their gains in the old setting. What Robert Marcus has described as a separation of state and national politics in the Republican party of the late nineteenth century generally characterized politics, level by level, throughout the century. Town, county, or city government had its own cast of competitors, its own range of possibilities, and its own labyrinth of rules. So did states, so did the national government. The advancing careers of even the most able professional politicians—Martin Van Buren, Abraham Lincoln, William McKinley—were a series of such choices. Although they capitulated with grace, they were nonetheless required to relinquish effective power in each smaller domain as they rose. The same was even true for anyone who moved out of a ward to become city boss late in the nineteenth century, and it at least stretched the abilities of those who tried to combine allegiance to a district or state on the one hand and a corporation on the other. The result was a complexity of ambitions and jurisdictions that dealt with one another like so many sovereign units, as sparingly as possible and always in the hope of drawing advantages from others to carry back into their own domains. ". . . [H]ow deep the division of the country into self-governing commonwealths goes," James Bryce wrote late in the century, "making men feel they have a right to do what they will"—what they could—within their bailiwicks.

The twentieth century superimposed a system of economic and social functions on this older pattern of geographical jurisdictions. Everything from home mortgages and public schools to agricultural marketing and airplane manufacture came in time within administrative spheres that were sufficiently separate from the legislatures creating them to constitute distinct realms of their own. Because the new system increasingly monopolized the politics of opportunity, it not only drained vitality from the traditional scheme of geographical layers but also softened their lines of exclusiveness. Almost any development undertaken in a town or city would involve an approval, often a continuing cooperation from some outside agency. Yet the details of local politics, which at times seemed to involve only a few real estate and merchandising interests, remained important to that majority of Americans who still identified themselves through the places where they lived. Local and even state government served more and more as vehicles for cultural politics, as a means of defending those values that an intrusive functional system either ignored or opposed, and its officers were expected to have strong personal roots to the geographical unit they represented. As late as the 1960s, it required the name of Kennedy to defy this rule and float in from another state to become New York Senator. A lesser attraction such as Pierre Salinger failed even in California, where mobility was a public virtue.

Interaction between these two networks—the one functional and heavily economic, the other geographical and heavily cultural—depended upon the possibility of separating issues according to the special concern of each sphere. Neither the delicacy of an administrative genius nor the distinctions of a master metaphysician could accomplish it with any consistency. At best their relations resembled a begrudging truce with endless little grabbing maneuvers for advantage. A new public problem or political ambition—prohibition, New Deal relief, a military draft, civil rights—could turn the large gray area between them into a battleground. Many politicians themselves were torn in their loyalties. Within each scheme, moreover, the tendencies were strongly centrifugal. Cultural politics was by its nature particular and protective. Occasional forays against an enemy never altered its basic urge to defend the prerogatives of many small constituencies. Although functional politics had an appearance of breadth and integration, it also divided as best it could into discrete domains, special function by special function. Administrators in public education or road construction or communications control spun webs of familiarity and mutual interest within their own realm that bound them apart from other functional jurisdictions. Inside each administrative area, these strands then extended more naturally to counterparts in private life—officials in the Department of Agriculture with farm groups, agents for military procurement with company executives—than they did from bureau to bureau across the charts of government. A vast increase in the incidence of human contacts made twentieth-century politics no less committed to compartmental autonomy, no less segmented than its predecessors.

One consequence of this political tradition was an impressive openness. From the adventurers who played colonial politics for their fortunes to the community promoters of the nineteenth century and the aspirants in the primary campaigns of the twentieth, shrewd and ambitious Americans found politics a particularly inviting avenue for advancement. The interstitial looseness of American society meant that almost any white male who could adapt and maneuver and lead would find a place for his talents. Rising groups, like individuals, also experienced relatively little resistance when they calculated their choices intelligently, for the politics of segmentation offered an exceptional range of options, a broad set of alternative units or levels or specialized sectors where resourceful new arrivals might establish themselves.

What politics expressed, government reflected. Over the centuries the most useful image of government was that of an empty vessel, a container into which power flowed and formed but which provided nothing of its own. Always an exaggeration, especially so by the mid-twentieth century, the image nevertheless expressed an approximate truth of high importance. Governments in each century did fix certain requirements for entry: the styles of patrician leadership in the eighteenth, the maintenance of parties in the nineteenth, the prerogatives of bureaucracy in the twentieth. But once these were met, government proved remarkably responsive. Groups received in rough proportion to the power they brought. This axiom set the pattern of assistance for community development, the boons to corporations, the privileges for occupations, the ways of a system that accommodated organized crime much as it did organized medicine or organized labor.

American political power, in other words, was particular rather than general, and attempts to marshal it for broad purposes were not merely frustrating but almost certainly futile. That was the fate of grand hopes for mobilization dating from Alexander Hamilton and Albert Gallatin to John Kennedy and George McGovern. It was the lesson that lay behind the sharp defeats of Thomas Jefferson, Woodrow Wilson, and Franklin Roosevelt, Presidents whose initial successes relied upon the principle of the government as clearing house and whose failures with the Embargo, the League of Nations, and the renovation of the Supreme Court and the Democratic party tried to implement very different assumptions about political power. In a smaller domain, the odds for mobilization were also poor. Even the legendary authority of the city boss was sharply limited by a crazy quilt of conflicting local bailiwicks and expectations that often turned urban politics, in Norton Long's phrase, into an "ecology of games." Those leaders in the early nineteenth century who dreamed of state planning, as the experiences of Ohio and New York demonstrated, fell prey almost immediately to the ravages of particularistic politics. In the mixed economic enterprises of those years, public representation was little more than a euphemism for another special interest, and its transfer to private control around mid-century, while signaling important changes in the techniques of finance, marked no revolution in power. Government subsidies to canals or railroads or highways or airlines that claimed to have a public purpose could only promise vague, general services through the alchemy of an enlightened particular interest.

Because elites did enjoy relatively easy access to government, they invited myths about a power that was enveloping everything. Each century saw absurdity in the fears of a preceding one—a nineteenth-century Whig laughed at Jefferson's nightmare of impending monarchy in the 1790s, a twentieth-century academician laughed at John Quincy Adams' vision of an insidious Masonic league in the 1830s—but each century then replaced them with its own images of a power elite. In part, weaker citizens created such myths because they found it less humiliating to retreat before an irresistible monolith than just a stronger opponent. In part, these images were tautological means of criticizing the current state of the nation. Revelations about the special privileges that major corporations commanded from modern government were often nothing more than complaints that success by American standards brought success in American society. Most important, these demonic visions expressed a fierce, traditional jealousy about power. It required very little evidence to expand this instinctive suspicion into the conviction that a favored few acted without any of the limitations bedeviling ordinary citizens.

Yet the members of a modern elite lived according to the same tradition of mutual distrust as other Americans. They too hoarded their special privileges, their compartmental sovereignties, and they struggled bitterly among themselves over who should be President, whether budgets should be large or small, how government agencies should be shaped and empowered. The jungle of bureaucratic conflict that had been Washington since the 1930s mirrored the suspicious, self-serving nature of these warring constituencies. Because the federal government was not designed to execute broad domestic policies, even an extensive economic power did not allow elite groups to establish systematic social controls. The wholesale viciousness toward dissenters between 1917 and 1924, and again between 1947 and 1954, revealed its meaning through a striking decentralization. Rather than implementing an elite's master plan, it expressed cruelties that were spread throughout America. An elite monopolized power segment by segment, came to the government group by group, and almost always received their exceptional benefits piece by piece. If they made the system work for them, they did so side by side, not together.

This general diffusion was a basic source of continuity in American society. Particularistic politics frustrated the ambitions of every potential power elite. People vilified and harassed and sporadically attacked their enemies, but they could very seldom gather a systematic force to crush the opposition. Until the mid-twentieth century, when a standing military power was placed at the executive's disposal, a mobilization for extensive foreign ventures was almost as unnatural. Imagine, for example, what Theodore Roosevelt might have done astride a different government. It was equally rare for the government to shape the outcome of private contests for power. The role of government was to reflect, not correct. During the nineteenth century, a revolution in the functions of the corporation transformed it from an indispensable means for gathering scattered capital to a device for maximizing the benefits from large capital reserves. A great many citizens, sensing a profound change, expressed it not unreasonably in charges of gambling and monopoly and financial chicanery, but their clamor had neither consistency nor organization. Haltingly, government at different levels adapted to the revolution without significantly altering its course. When a pattern of restraints did emerge in the twentieth century, it developed through innumerable competitions for privilege and protection in a fluid economy, as various groups demanded a corner here, a slice there, of the expanding modern system. It was these piecemeal struggles, not liberal principles or grand countervailing forces, that defined the boundaries of corporate power. Although government might intervene to lessen the conflict, or occasionally to preserve the rights of its own bureaucracy, ultimately it ratified the results.

No one took charge of American politics. Victory came to the tireless builder of temporary alliances, such as Martin Van

Buren or Lyndon Johnson, and the skillful disrupter of opposing alliances, such as Thurlow Weed or Richard Nixon.
From a distance, the sweep of politics created the impression
of a peculiar American moderation—pragmatic in style, realistic in objectives, conservative in defeat—and the rare prominence of an ideologue or a megalomaniac seemed only to
highlight the fundamentally temperate character of political
life. On the contrary, segmentation encouraged both absolutism and harshness. Within each unit, monopoly power was
the one natural goal, and any representative who adopted a
compromising approach revealed a weak commitment to the
cause. When leaders returned with less than everything, they
were sent out again to win the rest. The clash of absolutes in
an arena of uncertain alliances made every incremental advantage a precious one, and the usual application of this principle was to attack those somewhat weaker, to maximize
strength at the expense of an available, vulnerable group.
The more open the contest, the more the heads of others became the steps to success. Only an inability to seize the whole
loaf, not a willingness to accept half, limited the consequences of this bitter scramble.

Such incessant battling placed an extraordinarily high premium on brokerage. In order to serve this primary need,
political parties were organized early in the nineteenth century as state governments, one by one, were inundated with
schemes for local development. Political agents, most of whom
operated from a state capital, found that by sorting and combining these demands, they could give some order in the legislative pit and at the same time create at least temporary
clusters of mutual interest. As these clusters were modified to
express the values of cultural segmentation as well, parties
emerged. The pressures requiring the professional broker
also defined his role. He had to apportion benefits in ways appropriate to the nineteenth-century assumptions of insular,
parallel growth, yet maintain allegiance to a party. If he

treated each transaction as an independent affair, he would undermine the continuities of party and government. If he sought to integrate these diverse ambitions, he would lose the support of his constituents. Sustaining an acceptable tension between the two required perpetual attention and delicate skill, a diligent shrewdness that became the trademark of nineteenth-century political leadership.

The nineteenth-century professional had tried to distribute benefits so that scattered groups would remain together; his counterpart in the twentieth tried to distribute rewards so that crowded groups could remain apart. What geography and communication had built into the nineteenth century became the crucial synthetic creation of the twentieth. In the nineteenth century, agents for so many dispersed communities and interests had come like delegates from foreign lands to the centers of distribution and bargained with the managers. Because the demands for insularity were equally strong in the compact society of the twentieth century, managers were now required to erect barriers that would divide the participants without snarling the process of brokerage. As these complicated issues of separation came to cover larger and larger portions of American society, they heightened the importance of bipartisan councils—the inner club of the Senate, for example—and any other devices that might stabilize and coordinate the massive problems of distribution.

During the nineteenth century, it had paid to come early to a legislature. Even professional brokers had usually abided by the principle of first-come first-serve: a string of decisions until the money was gone, then perhaps a few more. In the twentieth, the models at least were a budget and a chart: some means of total apportionment expressing relative importance and some sense of the interrelated effects from these various benefits. In the process, however, brokers were expected to combine demands that were fundamentally irreconcilable. Elites increasingly insisted upon long-term arrangements suitable to their concern for predictable stability—what elites called public policy—while groups outside that circle tended to expect a more immediate return—what elites called pork barrel or handouts. In one more demonstration of the vertical gap in modern society, politicians faced charges of corruption when they authorized general frameworks of power for elites and charges of corruption when they allocated specific funds for other people's short-term benefits.

The broker acquired a new meaning as intermediary in the compact society of the twentieth century. Across a nation of distant competitors, political intermediaries had once filled an obvious need. Now in more contrived and elaborate ways, they adapted to serve equally as links and as buffers, not only negotiating differences but sealing adjacent units as much as possible from any direct encounter. Listening, offering, leaving, returning as they shuttled from group to group, brokers were required to settle issues of apportionment so that the groups themselves never met. The range of these problems —among varieties of business, between employers and employees, among ethnic groups, along the borderlines of organized medicine or established banking facilities—meant that all kinds of mediators, from prominent citizens and professional arbitrators to government commissions and special courts of law, spread a network of protective management around America's segments. Nothing better exemplified the new style of politics than the standard campaign tour: a public address and a private exchange of promises with each constituent group in turn, and the candidate as traveling intermediary, the sole common link among these many bargains. Even if the stops along the way were only a few blocks apart—perhaps especially if they were—the same formula prevailed. The purpose of America's conglomerate major parties was not simply the absorption of conflicts but their resolution without actual interaction among the competing groups.

Particularly in the twentieth century, Americans expected the dynamics of group competition to hide beneath the surface of politics. What coalition governments elsewhere told about the state of a bargaining process Americans considered too dangerous to exhibit. Lower houses of the legislature, where clashes frequently accompanied the business of the day, ranked as the least reputable branch of government. Displays of abrasion and struggle were almost always signs of failure. Just as a prospect of contending groups suddenly, explosively meeting face to face gave the convention of a major party its electric atmosphere, only the assumption of an eventual reunion enabled its partisans to tolerate the excitement. When third parties did materialize, they represented a special menace to public calm, a danger that differences once bared could jeopardize an entire scheme of covert management. By spotlighting factional conflicts, such Presidential candidates as Robert LaFollette and the two Wallaces became in an important sense public enemies. Hence the complaints that the major parties failed to formulate clear policies, that their competition was a noisy sham, actually complimented them on their efficiency. They seemed evasive because evasion was one of their principal tasks. Where the most desirable solution to conflict was invisibility, their bland platforms and pompous debates communicated well-being. Rather than the captives of consensus or the victims of anti-intellectualism, they were the rational agents of a segmented society.

Payoff served as the foundation for America's scheme of politics. Although the communities of the nineteenth century fixed their boundaries in ethnic and cultural terms, they defined their ambitions overwhelmingly in economic terms, and it was the outward thrust of these ambitions that required professional brokers and generated a system of parties. In time these parties came to fulfill other important functions as well. They ran lines of communication among the parts of society when little else connected them, and in the process they facilitated a multitude of transactions that extended well beyond the usual political concerns. They acted as the carriers of certain basic values that large numbers of citizens could accept as common American beliefs. They protected the cultural integrity of many compartments, including relatively weak ones. They managed the election of Presidents in a manner that made it difficult for a few groups to dominate the office and therefore freed it to serve the purposes of national cohesion. But the sustenance of the nineteenth-century system, its steady, daily source of strength, was the distribution of economic benefits—as large as a transcontinental railroad, as small as a bucket of coal.

As in so many areas of nineteenth-century society, the parties could never have thrived outside a climate heavy with indifference. However hectic the rush for favors sometimes became, it was manageable because most citizens most of the time directed their energies elsewhere. Under normal circumstances, the nineteenth-century preoccupation with cultural matters eased the strain on party management. Although these issues were intimately entwined with politics, they usually required exhortation—a pose of unswerving orthodoxy, a chant of truth. The skills of the broker had little applicability to clashes among these hard cultural commitments, and the health of any political party demanded that it rarely attempt to negotiate them. A sharply rising curve of such total politics in the 1850s paralyzed the professional brokers, crippled both major parties, and opened the way a bit wider to civil war; and a partial revival in the 1890s spread sufficient havoc to hasten the development of a new political system.

From another vantage point, the limited need for brokerage in the nineteenth century simply expressed in its own way the extraordinary wealth of the nation. An assumption that America offered multiple opportunities and that today's losers could be tomorrow's winners underpinned the entire system. It provided an indispensable leeway to the brokers, enabling them to play hopes against actual benefits and to decrease the intensity of bargaining across an extended schedule of anticipation. With confidence in abundance, communities could indulge their obsessions with cultural purity instead of forever badgering the brokers.

Even more important, abundance gave substance to the dream of parallel enterprise. Economic growth that did not necessitate head-to-head competition did not require the perpetual services of an intermediary. A withering of that faith among large numbers in the South and North framed the issue of secession, then encouraged a resort to war; an increasingly widespread belief late in the century that a privileged few could prosper only at the expense of the many signaled the fall of the nineteenth-century system. Above all, this fundamental assumption discouraged a centralization of the powers to allocate. The dream of plenty for everyone with the talent to seize it scattered people's attention, just as a fixed and niggardly total would have turned all eyes on each priceless chance and forced a radically different means of apportionment. Not only were brokers in a bountiful land asked to manage a relatively small percentage of its opportunities, but much of their task was seen as a removal of restraints, a broad yet elementary preparation for countless private ventures. Even at times of acute worry, that charge remained uppermost, and politicians hotly debated the right method of sweeping away some unnatural barrier to everybody's enterprise. Because the elimination of slavery lent itself to this kind of neat, legal solution, nineteenth-century politics could survive the Civil War. If the concentration of capital resources could have been dissolved by a similar formal device, that system of politics would not have collapsed when it did.

Twentieth-century America tightened the system of brokerage and relied much more self-consciously on abundance as the source of successful politics. A compact society of proliferating units required more than just an increasingly central direction. Elites now demanded a guarantee of benefits over long periods of time. These arrangements might authorize a legal monopoly in medicine with broad freedom in establishing fees, a cooperative oligopoly in steel with tacit assurances of judicial benevolence, a closed shop in university teaching with control over the passage to certification, or any of a multiplying number of variations. In each case, however, the same basic rules applied: a segment empowered to supervise its own jurisdiction and organize its own scheme of rewards. Although these arrangements required more and more government involvement, including subsidies, central management was almost as elusive as ever. The structure of the system was a series of contracts, whose negotiation, amendment, and maintenance comprised the core of elite politics, and any attempt at planning had to accept this accumulation as inviolable in all except its details. Government served primarily as the underwriter, secondarily as the coordinator, rarely as the integrator, never as the architect.

The operations of the system suggested a crowd in the bank who were selecting tellers according to the various certificates and checks they carried. Silently they stood in lines, occasionally wondering what transactions occurred at another window, mostly anticipating their turn ahead. As a certificate was honored or a check cashed, a social contract was fulfilled. Although there were notices around the bank about the responsible ways of using money, no one regarded these as more than advice, a matter quite apart from the contract. What did command attention was an argument over the validity of a certificate or a check. Everywhere people craned to hear, and those in the same line broke ranks to crowd around the window—some examining their own slips, others shouting, all very agitated until the issue was settled. Because too many of these incidents would destroy the whole order of business, the directors of the bank tried to ensure that no more than one occurred on the same day.

Waiting mutely in line required a basic confidence in the bank's reserves. American competition had always rested upon more for everybody rather than redistribution, and an absolute prerequisite for this tight system was a faith that the total for division would regularly, predictably expand, that any contraction or even stabilization was merely a moment's pause. The nation's leading brokers acquired direct responsibility for economic expansion. A popular belief in their ability to make the economy perform miracles, in fact, marked them as leaders, and all of them became specialists in the incantations of economic development and the manipulations of public feeling about it. No political leader could seriously propose, as detached critics did from time to time, that America worship some idol other than growth: a whole system was predicated on it. Franklin Roosevelt no less than Herbert Hoover had to see prosperity around the corner. Although anything was preferable to depression, a rampant inflation also created severe strains. Not even a booming economy could exact its price. As in Lewis Carroll's caucus race, everyone should win with prizes for all.

Because the total did expand so impressively, the system worked well despite its hazards. Even in depression it was possible to accommodate such large new units as the industrial unions, and the narrow range of debates among almost all participants about too little and too much verified how thoroughly they were committed to the fundamentals of American distribution. Groups held for a time on the edges of the system, once fully inside it, proved just as loyal as the veterans. Appropriate to its complex pattern of multiple boundaries and mutual suspicions, the many specific shifts in advantage brought no revolution in apportionment. During the first half-century of the modern system, as Gabriel Kolko has demonstrated, the poor did not become proportionately richer despite liberal claims of a new economic justice. Nor in a significant way did the rich grow proportionately richer despite the obvious leverage they enjoyed.

Instead, the nation grew richer, as more and more units formed lines of strangers, all eyes ahead, anticipating bigger payoffs.

Innumerable contracts with these subdividing segments spread inefficiencies throughout a system whose arrangements were fundamentally social rather than economic. To place compartmental autonomy and insular peace above economic rationality—yet remain prosperous—was a luxury of America's unprecedented wealth. It was that leeway which allowed Americans, decade by decade, to jerrybuild an assortment of uneasy solutions to the problem that the modern system was least equipped to meet: payoff by cultural criteria. Nineteenth-century distribution had automatically honored ethnic and cultural standards, for these lay at the center of social organization. Mugwumpish complaints about the boss and his immigrant clients, for example, had merely stated a preference for one set of cultural credentials over another; they had not provided an alternative rationale. Even when the modern system did develop a new occupational standard for distribution, the issue between old and new values remained unclear as long as the emerging elite themselves intermingled ethnic with occupational tests. Elevating a Jew, Louis D. Brandeis, to the Supreme Court in 1916 outraged a host of successful Americans. Then as the elite lost their ethnic sensitivity, they increasingly tried to ignore its lingering effects. A generation after the Brandeis appointment, they talked only in private about a Jewish seat on the court. Now the needs of a modern political economy supplied the one legitimate measure for a new Justice. Ethnic rewards belonged in a distasteful realm of local option, much as prostitution or pornography or parochial education did.

Upon this unformulated division rested the initial resolution to the problem of ethnic payoff. It was politically impossible to disregard the cultural values that a majority of Americans still used in the organization of their lives. Yet wherever an elite predominated, they would no longer honor these values. Because America was such a rich nation, it could support an elite system nationally and at the same time allocate funds that would be disbursed by ethnic and cultural criteria through state and local governments. A part of the New Deal's success—a success that created a long-term Democratic majority—derived from its regularization of this compromise, sometimes simplified as Franklin Roosevelt's willingness to bargain with conservative southerners and city bosses.

However reasonable to most professional brokers, this arrangement remained dirty politics to leaders of the national elite, who stubbornly refused to acknowledge its right to a place in the system. The least they demanded was its strict containment. By the 1930s they were embarking on a route that in the early 1960s would bring many of them full circle, this time to welcome national surveillance over ethnic and cultural issues because of the extremely low rather than the high priority they assigned such values. Inevitably they encountered the structure of ethnic payoff with the deepest and most open tradition: black segregation. Successful Americans of every variety had participated in its operation, consistently sacrificing changes there to something else that ranked above it on their agendas. Much as Gentiles had once lectured Jews at the height of anti-Semitism, elite whites had told blacks that whatever the disabilities of segregation, they were doing better in a wealthy America than they could anywhere else— that a bit of American payoff, in other words, should suffice. It was reasonable enough, therefore, for an arch-segregationist such as James Byrnes of South Carolina to declare in the 1950s that the logical answer to an economically impoverished system of black schools was an economically enriched system of black schools. Few American traditions, after all, could match the authority of a payoff by color. In the 1960s, it was also difficult to refute arguments for the new allocations that some blacks demanded as a compensating distribution. Nevertheless, white leaders who were committed to the irrationality of ethnic payoffs in general found black capitalism and its companion programs little more acceptable than segregation, and in national affairs they gave as grudgingly as they could. The Chicanos and Indians who followed with comparable appeals were rejected without even the soothing rhetoric. Cultural groups could either aspire to a life of elite values or take their places in a constricted scheme of local benefits. Although the members of certain groups now had much freer access to that elite world, the basic formula of the 1970s, after years of confusion and upheaval, looked remarkably similar to the original compromise of the 1930s.

Ethnic minorities were told in effect to join the game and play by its rules. During the nineteenth and twentieth centuries that process largely defined the terms of assimilation for any new group seeking entry to American society. In a nation of segments, the surrogate for mutual trust was a common set of rules, a unity through procedures, and an acknowledged place in the system required their unambiguous acceptance. American males learned early that life was not like a game, it was a game: a race, a contest, a match of one's abilities against opportunity, a measure of effective team work. What a decent world would provide them was a guarantee of determinate rules, clear and open, so that each unit—an individual or community, a business venture or occupational group—could enter the game with confidence. The heart of the message was neither sportsmanship—the fair play of British tradition—nor a gamble—the fated turn of a roulette wheel. Americans expected an honest game, explicitly stated and impartially supervised, and where it was in doubt, they cheered promises of a Square Deal, a New Deal, a Fair Deal —an improved version of the social contract.

More than a cynical hypocrisy led successful Americans to demand that losers continue to abide strictly by the rules, and more than a vague national optimism kept so many losers in competition. The game was the American way, a compelling requirement that affected people quite apart from a cool assessment of its odds. Refusing to play was a dangerous option, for much of society's security rested upon the game's inclusiveness, and abstainers as well as dissenters faced severe penalties. Early in the nineteenth century, and again early in the twentieth, the confusions and recriminations attending a major shift in the game expressed this widespread dependence upon a sense of absolute, unquestioned rules. Even winners in a new system were extremely reluctant to admit that the traditional game had altered, more because of the high risks any general change entailed than because of a personal conservatism or a desire to dupe the losers. If a common game dissolved, what else would hold the participants together?

With so few alternatives for defining social relationships, Americans had shown a constant, almost obsessive concern for political and legal forms. Since the seventeenth century, that concentration on forms had allowed disparate groups to maintain contact even when they could not speak with each other. Where a folk spirit or a mystic state had no applicability, a structure of rules and procedures served in their stead as a critical mode of comprehension, a manner of gauging security at home and evaluating the world beyond. It was a persuasion that created wide audiences for Locke and Montesquieu but almost none for Rousseau, that gave American society a contractual bent well before nineteenth-century capitalism. Intimations that a framework of rights and rules was less than immutable transformed colonists into British dissenters, then revolutionaries. A purification of forms dominated public debate in the age of the founding fathers, provided the rationale for Jacksonian reforms, justified policy in both North and South during the era of the Civil War, supplied the logic for progressivism, suffused the arguments of the New Deal, and sanctioned participation in two world wars. Without proper forms there could be no liberty on the European continent during the eighteenth century, in Latin America during the nineteenth, or in the Soviet Union during the twentieth. How neighboring Canada could claim to be as free as the United States inside the loose, negotiable arrangements of the British Commonwealth simply eluded Americans. These involvements, as Americans understood them, were neither liberal nor conservative. By establishing a precondition without determining a purpose, a structural approach could accommodate a wide range of impulses, and the most daring as well as the most cautious proposals were somehow fitted within the indispensable forms. Only the very few who attacked the forms themselves, who called them useless or inherently warped, placed themselves outside the debate. Anarchy conjured a special horror to Americans.

The first, clear concepts of the United States as a nation expressed this deep dependence upon structure. In the early years of the nineteenth century, when most loyalties originated locally and expanded reluctantly, the need for a determinate frame had already made the nation critically important. Strands of ambition ran in every direction throughout the land. Outsiders as well as Americans populated the country. The nation, like an enveloping presence, would contain that mass of otherwise random, amoral behavior. In this abstract sense of a restraining form, the nation acquired a sacred meaning which the legal debates of the antebellum period and the decision in the South to establish a separate structure did not fundamentally shake. Because chaos was the alternative to a properly designed outer structure, Americans battled with a special passion to determine the correct one. In retrospect, Lincoln's judgment that the Union had never been broken—could not have been broken—was the necessary American interpretation of secession and civil war. If the form really had cracked, all would have disintegrated. Inside a secure framework, Southerners and Northerners, if they chose, could still view each other as aliens without jeopardizing an ultimate order. Although this inclusive structure became much more concrete, much more intimately related to the procedures of a national system in the twentieth century, an essentially metaphysical quality always remained. Even a modern elite required the comfort that only an overarching form could provide.

To encase their structure, Americans required a soft, tough cover of fundamental law that would contain without crowding a society of segments. During the sharp debates in the first century of the republic, this was the promise made in behalf of both the common law and a singularly American codification: firm but adaptable. It was the goal of those who sought to escape some rigid legal principle through appeals to the Declaration of Independence or a higher law, a tactic neither rare nor radical in the nineteenth century. It lay behind the urge to establish a minimum of basic rights for all adults—to hold property, to receive a fair trial, perhaps to vote—so that a national system could include everyone without at the same time making them equals or even necessarily Americans. If blacks were given the franchise, for instance, it would qualify them as participants in a system but certainly not as full members of American society.

It was this powerful need for a legal sheath that gave the Constitution its extraordinary reputation. Although its creators had not sought elasticity, they did wish to grant leaders a very broad leeway in applying true principles, and their phrasing allowed the latitude that Americans over the next two centuries required. National and therefore inclusive, written and therefore definitive, general and therefore malleable: these were magnificent qualifications that Americans were already discerning in the lifetime of the founders, and early in the nineteenth century they elevated the Constitution to holy rank. The Confederacy, dedicated to an even purer version of scripture, copied almost every word to contain its own compartmentalized society. Neither the struggles to amend the Constitution nor an occasional assault from intellectuals could significantly affect its unique reputation, for nothing could replace its unique service.

This adulation, in turn, was the source of the Supreme Court's special place in American society. A final arbiter of national law was indispensable, one given to epigrammatic rulings was certainly attractive, and one with the weakest links to implementation was in the end irresistible. Far better than any available alternative, the Supreme Court could sustain that magic combination of authority and flexibility, the last word and the least power to enforce it. Although its reputation varied erratically, its function always remained to be fulfilled, and even the most acute problems surrounding it dissolved before this necessity. The Marshall Court from time to time alienated large sections of the population without in the end diminishing its importance, and a year after the Dred Scott decision, Lincoln found himself on the defensive when he seemed to impugn the prerogatives of the court. Neither Roosevelt could translate his popularity into an effective assault on its privileges. The most successful attacks charged the court with violating the basic law that it was obligated to uphold, but the argument's inherent vagueness and the court's adaptability usually blunted even this opposition. Like the Constitution it manipulated, the court provided services to a segmented society that simply could not be matched elsewhere.

Hard law was equally as critical as soft. Americans calculated their everyday well-being by the clarity of lines between compartments, and these divisions the law also preserved. If the Constitution and Supreme Court guaranteed a common American game, an array of very specific laws provided the rules by which participants must play. The former would hold them together, the latter apart. A strong inclination to litigate was already evident in the seventeenth century, and by the eighteenth a disputatious involvement with legal details had become crucial to the truce among strangers inside the heterogeneous colonies. The preoccupation with law that struck Alexis de Tocqueville early in the nineteenth century drew upon a rich heritage. It was appropriate that twentieth-century America would serve as an international center for the study of sophisticated administration. In a society of jealous, interdependent segments, minds sharpened to plot every division and catch every nuance of authority were a wise investment, and people from around the world came to learn from the American experts.

In lieu of a residual good will or a traditional understanding stood an extraordinarily elaborate book of rules. It was a system for lawyers, who became not merely the translating technicians but the dominant figures in American politics. Judges, rather than simply the agents of order, were indispensable referees in a vital and ragged game. Legal specialists commanded respect, not love. Necessity elevated their functions without exalting the practitioners. What American would consistently applaud an opponent's clever player—or the referee? Hostility toward the wily advocate and his intricate law ran throughout American history, and American utopias almost always eliminated both.

Hard law generated such strong feelings because it contained a primary tension between law as protection and law as intrusion. The formula distinguishing the two was already quite clear by the eighteenth century, as puzzled Englishmen learned in the 1760s from the colonial differentiation between external and internal authority. Law should negotiate, clarify, and preserve the divisions among autonomous segments. Its role stopped at the segment's boundaries; inside, the members regulated their own lives. They might voluntarily grant certain rights in the larger public interest, and occasionally they might even invite an outside agency to assist in their local affairs. In neither case, however, did they consider the prerogatives of compartmental autonomy diminished.

Over the centuries, this ideal received an impressive substantiation. By the revolutionary era it was expressed in many variations of religious and civil self-government, then embodied in a Bill of Rights. It underwrote the Jeffersonian system. By the nineteenth century it had expanded to include a far more complex administrative network. Reliable local people would represent the state and federal government at home, wear the sheriff's badge and walk the policeman's beat, and generally oversee everyday life. The sanctity of trial by jury derived from its judgment not by peers but by dependable neighbors who would uphold the community canons. This concept of justice also required a local adaptation of external rules—a community translation of land laws or public school provisions or tax assessments. Americans surely had "an obligation to the laws," Andrew Jackson wrote in 1835, "but a higher one to the communities in which we live."

In the twentieth century the impermeable core of sovereignty remained, segment by segment, the right to set and supervise internal standards. When Lieutenant Colonel Anthony Herbert, the perfect soldier by a literal reading of the army manual, tried to hold his superiors to the written word on war crimes in the 1960s, millions in the trade unions and the investment firms and the hospital staffs recognized immediately why he was so harshly ostracized. They too had customary ways that must never be exposed to an outsider's judgment. At a distance the details of how people conducted these affairs seldom roused much emotion. Even corporate price fixing or partisan spying, General Electric's executive criminals in 1960 or Watergate's political criminals in 1972, could not, as isolated incidents, touch the same popular nerve that rioting or bank robbing did. Rather than real crimes, they seemed more exposés of how others lived. They poked no holes in the legal mesentery of a segmented society.

While broad agreement from century to century sustained the ideal, an equally impressive tradition of conflict revealed the ambiguity of law in American society. A part of that tradition was rarely articulated, because marginal Americans, who enjoyed the protection of the law only when more powerful people allowed it, seldom entered the debate over its threatening implications. But where power was more diffuse or more evenly distributed, the effects of the law defined the nation's major problems in public policy. Did the Alien and Sedition Acts against Jacobinical infection protect or intrude? The answer required a bitter nationwide struggle and the pivotal election of 1800. Did the Second Bank of the United States preserve or destroy the channels of community expansion? National parties organized around the issue. Did the laws supplementing slavery maintain or undermine community sovereignty? Americans resolved the question in civil war. Did the elementary rights of blacks fall inside or outside the domain of federal law? A military occupation of the South hinged on the answer. Should the law defend large corporations as new units in parallel competition or subordinate them to community enterprise? Nineteenth-century society crumbled when it could not rephrase the question. Did national prohibition increase or erode the strength of America's segments? A modern system could not function effectively until that kind of question was discarded. Were the civil rights of all citizens a federal or compartmental responsibility? An inability to parcel the issue exposed, then widened the fissures in American society at midcentury.

Policies were framed in terms of division and impingement because the clarity and strength of boundaries defined their meaning. From Condorcet's bewilderment at the large fears over Shays' little rebellion to European horror at the ferocity of American antiradicalism in the 1950s, outsiders mistook a preoccupation with problems of law and order for neurotic overreaction. Crucial issues naturally elicited powerful emotions. The very agreement among Americans that their society could not survive without a strict adherence to the book of rules made their debates over its contents so combustible.

Where everybody had so much at stake, miscalculations in policy were inevitable, and the consequences predictable: a brittle conviction that society's survival depended upon the enforcement of the law set against an equally brittle conviction that its enforcement would destroy society. Times of general conflict such as the 1850s and 1960s differed from the normal pattern of smaller encounters only in visibility and scope. Always the line separating law and order from law and disorder, law from lawlessness, was exceedingly fine. A small shift in perspective, a slight adjustment in the weight of priorities, could transform the defense of a community's autonomy into anarchy, or the protection of social divisions into an assault on liberties. Leaders who failed to sense the subtle changes might preside in blind innocence over a disintegrating peace.

The primary responsibility for all leaders with a mixed constituency was maintenance. Whether they presided over a city or a nation, they were expected above all to serve as chief broker and as keeper of law and order, and their discretion was tightly circumscribed by these obligations to facilitate transactions and sharpen lines. Before the 1930s, leaders were not automatically blamed for depressions, but they could rarely succeed in the midst of hard times because smaller allocations almost by definition made them failures. If they could ease the entry of new groups into the political system without disrupting it, they won special acclaim. Great Presidents were remembered for minimizing damage during difficult transitions: Jefferson for the revolution that did not follow his election; Jackson for his ability to avoid an eruption over nullification; Lincoln for his restraint in piloting a contentious North through the Civil War and offering hopes of unity beyond; Franklin Roosevelt for his inspired guidance along the middle of the road. Outstanding leadership of this sort came to be judged practical or pragmatic. Because their se

constituent groups were so unyielding, leaders had to be so
flexible. Because the maintenance of divisions and contracts
was such a demanding absolute, any techniques in its behalf
were presumed legitimate. Only when leaders dealt with another jurisdiction—the mayor negotiating with the state, the
governor with the nation, the President with foreign powers
—were they praised for those obdurate, tenacious qualities
normally associated with spokesmen for the segments.

As overseer of the national game the President, like other
leaders, safeguarded separation and diversity; as symbol for
the nation he, unlike any other leader, expressed an ultimate
American unity. On the one hand he was the Chief Executive,
a larger version of a standard assignment; on the other he was
first citizen, a unique role. Of, yet apart from, his society, he
was set on a plane above the battles without severing a connection with them. He should be as coolly detached as the
mythical Washington yet as sensitively attuned to the feelings of the people as the fabled Lincoln. Because he derived his legitimacy from the people, he could only arrive
through the rough, scarring processes of electoral politics.
Once in office, however, he should be transformed. His behavior should remove him from the perpetual pushing for advantage, the endless particulars of political bargain and sale.
The President signified social harmony. Yet because he rose
from a specifically American society, he could not pretend, in
the sense of a De Gaulle or a Churchill, to *be* America. While
he united the nation, he did not embody it. Nor could he
violate its principles by translating the urge for cohesion into
a tight national mobilization toward concrete domestic goals.
Even as the symbol of wholeness he would have to preside,
not command.

As first citizen in a segmented society, the President gave a
peculiarly personal cast to national leadership. More than
a narrow involvement with politics made a so-called Presidential synthesis the standard means of comprehending the na-

tion's history. Americans named piece after piece of their past for its President because he alone could communicate a special quality of the moment, and they found foreign countries without such a focal leadership hard to understand, easy to condemn. Coups in Latin America, rapid changes of government in France, a troika in the Soviet Union were by definition proof of social turmoil. Retrospectively, each President seemed the sole man who could have held the office in his time, the one accurate reflection of his America. Even those who had wanted another candidate to win could only say in defeat that the tenor of the nation had required the wrong man. Successful Presidents presumably used that unique personal authority in ways fundamental to society's health—Washington containing the hostility between Jefferson and Hamilton, Lincoln abating tensions with a tall tale, the first Roosevelt settling a serious coal strike in his chambers, the second exorcising anger with an incomparable charm—and lesser Presidents were berated for their failure to make the crucial gesture or soothing mediation.

This set of assumptions about the President subtly shaded into the expectation that he would exercise a broad formative influence on the character of American society. To a great many New Englanders, Jefferson—not policies or party but the man—was the revolution of 1800. A "Black Republican" in the White House sped a singularly American message throughout the South in 1860, and a special vindictiveness toward Jefferson Davis represented an appropriate northern response to a hated cause. In mundane terms of force or legislation or votes, power was not the issue. Nor was it for the many Americans in 1960 who announced a new era of national energy after John Kennedy's fractional victory over Richard Nixon, or for the national commission at the end of the sixties that recommended a new moral leadership from President Nixon as its solution to the problem of discontented youth. The guiding assumption was an extraordinary capacity to condition society through personality, a Presidential mystique that did, in fact, affect Presidents even when the rest of the country remained intractable. The most committed partisans—Van Buren, Chester A. Arthur, Warren G. Harding—groped for higher ground from a conviction that one way or another they as individuals might determine the national temper. Little wonder that Americans resented iconoclastic attacks on their Presidential heroes. If Washington and Lincoln were ordinary mortals, who could hope to escape from passion and bias? And if no one was free, who would unify this nation of compartments and contracts?

Such a high calling required a very special cluster of qualities that Americans reshaped as their values and their conceptions of national government changed. During the first years of the republic, Presidents were to assume office as if they had been born to the cloth. They would stand atop the national hierarchy as natural leaders, whose breeding, learning, and discipline gave them an inner harmony capable of creating an optimum social harmony. It was the apparent absence of these characteristics in Jackson that caused the aging fathers to oppose his candidacy and that marked his election as the end of a Presidential era. In the nineteenth century, Presidents were expected to exemplify America's primary moral absolutes so that by their character they would preserve the nation's core of values. A President might use that inner toughness to shield the nation, as many believed Jackson did, or he might simply model the upright citizen's life, as William McKinley did. With a rapid increase in the responsibilities of the national government, Americans in the twentieth century sought a President who would personify the policy orientation they wanted of that government. Sometimes the accent fell on vitality—the energy of Theodore Roosevelt or the confident experimentation of Franklin—and sometimes on calm—keep cool with Coolidge, relax under Eisenhower's genial smile. Debates over style—Herbert Hoo-

ver or Al Smith, Kennedy or Nixon—communicated much
of what citizens expected from their Presidents.

In light of these special responsibilities, an obsession with
safe Presidential candidates made excellent sense. If he were
to preside successfully over an elaborate scheme of brokerage,
a candidate could not afford too close an identification with
any of the major competing units. In the nineteenth century,
when geography defined such a large proportion of the demands on government, party leaders studied the location of
candidates with an astrological intensity. An attachment to a
specific business interest effectively destroyed a candidate's
credentials. Even in the 1920s, with the reputation of business
at its height, Hoover shrewdly labeled himself an engineer
rather than an entrepreneur. All candidates, in other words,
sought the illusion of a neutral base. As long as the military
was not recognized as an important segment in its own right,
generals could appear as proven national leaders who stood
apart from the everyday struggles over payoff. Military glory
belonged to all Americans, and generals from Jackson to
Eisenhower seemed to glide into office without ties or commitments. Inherited wealth of an undifferentiated sort served
almost as well, once the Jacksonian battle against patrician
arrogance had well passed. What private economic ambitions
could a Roosevelt or a Kennedy be hiding?

A safe model for a heterogeneous nation required a comparable illusion of neutral social origins. For most of American history, that meant a blurred version of white Anglo-
Saxon Protestantism. Catholic candidates simply did not
appear during the nineteenth century, and by the 1920s the
reasons why had not sufficiently disappeared to let Al Smith
slip within acceptable bounds. As late as the 1960s it was crucial that no one could mistake the Kennedy accent for inner-
city Irish. No gloss whatsoever could qualify an avowed athe-
ist. In the twentieth century, members of an occupational
elite were particularly alert to a candidate's assimilation of

their values. They no longer found any charm in the rise from rags to riches; the poor now lived by values too dangerously at odds with those of the elite. As stable a political professional as Harry Truman never quite eliminated doubts that as a failure in small business he could not preside sympathetically over the modern system. This array of restrictions, indistinguishably American in one sense, applied with special force to the nation's center of maintenance and moral exemplification. A fear of gambling here usually transcended the need to calculate voting blocs and potential majorities. But for anyone who advocated a risk, the disastrous record of deviant candidates—Smith, Barry Goldwater, George McGovern—could serve as a practical reminder of the complexities of conformity.

No President escaped the tension between his responsibility for maintenance and his obligation to national unity. One task required the broker's manipulation of countless divisions and demands, occasionally the manager's intrusion in the name of law and order; the other a stance of benign disengagement. Beginning with Washington's second term, these pulls of involvement and detachment tugged in some fashion at each occupant. Of the first six Presidents only Jefferson found an effective relationship between national leadership and the usual irrelevance of government, and in the face of international crisis he also failed to abide by it. Although Presidents in the nineteenth century held fewer illusions about vigorous leadership, they in turn found it extremely difficult to reconcile the highly partisan setting of their office and their role of impartial overseer. Because their functions as chief broker were fulfilled through party channels, they had great difficulty finding a neutral area from which to speak. Until 1898 even war belonged to a party. What spared them greater trials was the very small amount of specific action normally expected of them. If their interventions in American society generally misfired, they were seldom invited to fail. From a distance, Lincoln could be recognized as the nineteenth-century President whose exceptional skills enabled him to survive by far the most complicated array of these challenges.

Twentieth-century society concentrated more and more burdens of maintenance upon the Presidency. The modern system of congested separateness, with its elaborate devices for payoff, increasingly relied upon services that in some fashion were guaranteed through executive departments and ultimately, therefore, by the President himself. Although the outlines of the new executive had developed gradually during the first quarter of the century, their implications, especially as they affected the President alone, did not fully emerge until the Great Depression—Hoover's responsibility and curse in a personal sense no previous President had ever experienced. The blunt slogan on Harry Truman's desk, "The Buck Stops Here," communicated a broad social message that Benjamin Harrison could never have understood. Even Nixon's extraordinary deficiencies as a national symbol of law and morality would not have swelled the movement for impeachment in 1974 if he had not also been exposed as a dishonest broker in a time of sudden shortages and severe inflation.

One result of these new responsibilities was to dilute the partisanship of the office. In an era when almost all of its tasks were petty ones, Americans had identified the President not merely by a party but even by a distinct faction within it. He alone had set the style of an administration in the nineteenth century. The partisan upheaval surrounding John Tyler's replacement of William Henry Harrison or Chester Arthur's replacement of James Garfield had been tolerable only because so few people were significantly affected by it. With a great deal at stake in the twentieth century, the federal bureaucracy that swelled grandly and spread throughout American society absorbed almost all of the impact from a change of Presidents. Truman succeeded Roosevelt and Eisenhower, Truman with scarcely a ripple in the system. Americans could no longer indulge a partisan domination of the executive.

While the traditional strains between partisan and public roles were easing, new ones associated with maintenance intensified. Nothing diminished the need for a single individual to stand guard above its parts. Yet one person could master only the smallest fraction of America's innumerable, complicated arrangements: in their most rudimentary form they had already exceeded the comprehension of Theodore Roosevelt. At the same time, a complete removal from details defied the self-discipline of every President who was tempted, from the lethargic William Howard Taft to Eisenhower the senior staff officer, for the controversial decision of a subordinate, as they knew, would eventually reach them. The more they lost themselves in particulars, the less they could ponder the broad requirements of the whole society— or at least adopt a pose of detached concern. When they assumed an impartial air, they were invariably implored to clarify lines and crystallize order with a sweeping dispatch only the President could execute. To ride a white horse in Buddha-like contemplation none could approximate. And if the President acted forcefully, encased as he was within an elite world, the likelihood increased each decade that his strong decision from the top would only weaken the system as it reached the bottom. Neither instant opinion polls nor lightning communication shortened distances that were conceptual rather than geographical. "A striking feature of the past dozen years," a prominent political scientist observed in 1961, "has been the extent to which expressions of alarm at the decline of presidential leadership have occurred simultaneously with expressions of alarm at the growth of executive power." An unmanageable cluster of expectations, each logical by its separate origins, had collected around an office no one could satisfactorily fill.

Every political leader with a varied constituency required

a justification of authority, and a framework of constitutions, charters, and legislation did not suffice. Who could specify the lines or arbitrate the differences unless the contending parties had in some manner empowered him as their broker? Who could represent the whole if a mere majority of scattered pieces had elected him? The only solution available in American society was the process of election. Neither family name, social class, nor prior experience could guarantee any prerogatives that had not been validated by the voters, and as a result, elections were scrutinized with a sacramental care once reserved for the entrails of the pigeon.

In order to surmount the limitations of a simple majority, political competitors accepted a composite meaning for elections that transformed thousands of individual votes into a collective voice. Although losers occasionally carped at the size or spread of an opponent's majority, as winners they also claimed the right to read their victory as the whole people's judgment, one that subsumed an entire electorate in its majority. When the people had decided upon a leader, minorities in effect disappeared. Elections did not require winners and losers to cooperate or factions to receive a partial representation, both frightening prospects in a nation of compartments. Winners took all, spoke for all.

So that elections could give precise answers, their meaning was narrowed whenever possible to the act of voting itself. The absence of violence or gross illegality—the usual American tests of health—sanctioned the procedure. Who had been eligible to vote, how many of those eligible had voted, how the voting districts had been drawn were all matters for debate at another time. The purpose of the ballot was an even more hazardous subject. Perhaps the vote had been a minor function of a community holiday, a small demonstration of friendship, a little bargain for personal gain, a ritual of good citizenship, a predetermined expression of the family's heritage; perhaps it had been a calculated choice between candidates. The secret ballot might have confused the meaning of the act or clarified it. At the hour for divination, no one asked. It was imperative to concentrate solely on the act, an event frozen in time that rendered an authoritative decision. In a segmented society elections were too precious a source of unity, too valuable a procedural cement, to risk a searching social analysis, and the few skeptics who tried found themselves talking to each other.

Every age devised special rites of justification from these elections. The eighteenth-century version was most simple and most dangerous. Confident of their right to rule, the founding fathers interpreted victory as a sign of their constituents' virtue, often a mirror image of instructions from the very men elected. Hence defeat indicated the spread of evil influences, a citizenry misguided by false leaders, and repeated defeats, by implying an incorrigible public, raised serious doubts about the system itself. Political leaders in the nineteenth century, on the other hand, could rarely afford to question the system. Lacking a sense of inbred prerogatives, now relying exclusively on a public mandate, they came to depend upon an abstraction variously called a just or rational or true public opinion, one that existed apart from a mere sum of votes. Sometimes only a handful of citizens abided by its standard. Then leaders found it necessary to act against the wishes of a numerical majority, on the assumption that a temporarily deluded electorate would in time reverse its own errors.

A wealth of information about voting blocs, and a cynical belief in the capacity to manipulate the electorate, complicated the search for the public in the twentieth century, but most Americans still managed to find it. The most common device was some variation on the principle of a true America —Anglo-Saxons, for instance, or property owners or consumers or those committed to a vaguely liberal philosophy. Others created a public through mathematical calculations, often highly elaborate schemes that balanced or cancelled the effects of conflicting groups in order to produce a formula of moderation not unlike the rational ideal of the nineteenth century. The standard résumé of an opinion poll, beginning with a statement of the national average and then showing how subgroups fit as parts of the whole, was one popular means of reinforcing the assumption of a single American public. Although it was sometimes difficult to interpret elections as a funnelling of innumerable interests through the ballot box into a mandate for leadership, it was an exercise in mental gymnastics no less necessary than it had been a century before.

The justification of leadership was further complicated by an expectation among Americans that leaders would indeed act in their behalf. "Under conditions of representative government," Hannah Arendt has written, "the people are supposed to rule those who govern them." By the mid-eighteenth century a traditional jealousy of local rights had established imprecise but crucial boundaries around the powers of leadership, and the importance of these boundaries made talk about the dissolution of a government contract, a return to nature, considerably more than bookish phrases. "They were all commanders," a member of the Fries uprising of 1799 in Pennsylvania was reported as saying. If no man represented them, every man would represent himself until a proper government could be established. In the nineteenth century these outer limits were redefined in terms of popular mandates, and the assumption of a direct commandment from the electorate to the elected raised hopes of an immediate change whenever a new candidate won. Although in part a self-fulfilling process that took its proof from the unique character of the victor, these expectations still gave political life a steady rhythm of anticipation and disappointment, a monotonous recapitulation of the same promises and the same excuses.

American politics consistently operated with a popular distrust of leaders. Elites from the days of Federalism to the era of Franklin Roosevelt cried a constant stream of warnings about the demagogic communion between leaders and masses. The conservative oligarchy, which almost always appeared safer to them than a lone, strong President, never seemed able to establish itself. Countless citizens either translated each move by a suspicious official into the first step toward dictatorship or dismissed all politicians as crooks. The first opinion poll to register a majority believing that Nixon had lied in his professions of ignorance about Watergate also reported four out of five judging him no more dishonest than his predecessors. The segmentation that required leaders for negotiation, maintenance, and symbolic unity also generated the fear that they would surely violate their calling.

Americans, as Europeans regularly reminded them, produced no systematic theory that could rank among the significant philosophical contributions to Western thought. Friends of the United States replied that Americans, on the contrary, excelled in practical, concrete matters: they adapted to an everyday world while others spun their cosmic designs. But many academic critics simply deplored an American antipathy to the play of ideas, an explicit anti-intellectualism that exposed the worst about a materialistic culture. What almost everyone failed to note was the critical role that theory did have in the workings of American society. Without a constant flow of abstractions and a citizenry attuned to receive them, that society could not have operated, and leaders of all kinds specialized in this form of communication.

Inductive reasoning only served Americans well in those social affairs where continuity and mutual trust allowed a pool of common information to develop. Although Americans did create such pools, segment by segment, each reservoir was limited to members only. To understand a world beyond the segment, Americans relied upon simple principles from which endless deductions could then be made. As de Tocqueville remarked in the midst of Jacksonian enterprise, Americans were singularly Cartesian in their manner of thinking. Then and later, their normal response to new information was taxonomic, and they sorted it according to a small set of abstractions.

This kind of theory had little use for the normal rules of internal consistency and overall structure. It fulfilled highly practical, daily needs, and it bent to accommodate them. Whatever strengthened a sense of mastery over the wider society found a place among the abstractions. If leaders could connect disparate groups with a simple absolute, it automatically satisfied an American logic. Because ideas had an immediate utility, because Americans depended upon theory to sustain a fragile unity, they demanded relevance from their abstractions. Above all else, their so-called anti-intellectualism resisted what seemed to them frivolities of the mind. They welcomed theory that helped them understand, that extended the thin network of cohesion, and they abruptly dismissed the rest. Their rejection of some uses for ideas derived not from a hostility to the abstract or a worship of the mundane but from a profound commitment to other uses for ideas.

Sculpted theory was a luxury of societies where people could take for granted the very qualities of organization and interaction that in America theory was asked to produce. The sweeping truths about law and elections and Presidential leadership belonged to that utilitarian scheme, as did the principles about liberty, equality, and opportunity. Foreigners tended to miss the crucial meaning behind the American claims to a unique society. Those boasts dealt fundamentally with the existence rather than the superiority of a society. They exalted America in order to create it.

# ~VI~

## *Consequences*

In times of discontent, Americans traditionally resisted the elementary proposition that every social system carries a composite price. They would not relinquish the hope of finding somewhere in the world that ideal remedy—European high culture, primitive South Seas happiness, mystical Asian peace —to cure their nagging pains. It was a delusion that segmentation encouraged, for the apparent sovereignty of each unit, the sense of a compartment's unique truth floating in an ocean of errors, seemed to allow dramatic improvements in isolation from the rest of society. But systems came whole. To yearn for a detached and responsible British aristocracy, as some Americans did from the eighteenth through the mid-twentieth century, was to welcome the class structure underlying it. The fantasy of a Bolshevik Revolution for America invited, among much else, an American Stalin to follow it, and a contemporary radical passion for China's version involved massive cultural importations defying the most elastic imagination. The challenge of any major change was always the high cost of wholesale change, and a decision to accept the challenge required, first of all, a close examination of the price a current system was exacting. From the perspective of the 1970s, the most profound consequences of a segmented society—the ones worth this hard calculation of price—were the weakness of an American public at home and the effect of American power abroad.

Public is a complicated concept. Basically it involves activities that all participants can voluntarily or at least customarily accept, and facilities that are open to an entire constituency. Hence public can neither come by fiat nor bring results that the participants cannot abide—say, prohibition in Milwaukee or Protestant education in a self-consciously Catholic ward. Nor can it be regulated by rules that have no relationship with its functions. Public medical services may be allocated by types of illness but not levels of status. A public park may be apportioned by interests—a ball diamond here, a picnic area there—but not by hair styles or skin colors. In America, public also excludes economic profit as a primary rationale and requires the tolerance of the law.

Existing in, not apart from the rest of society, a public realm contains the tensions of normal living and therefore its common agreement remains as contingent as the shifting attitudes of its constituents. Public expresses an inclination rather than a formal state of affairs; it appears in degrees. As a leaning, it is measurable along a continuum—a range of publicness—that registers certain qualities of public behavior without insisting upon the simultaneous presence of all components.

Throughout American history, segmentation squeezed public activities within exceptionally narrow limits. Arenas with a potential for common, open enterprise were treated as a vacuum, an unclaimed region to preempt before others filled it, and indeterminate control over these spaces generated deep anxieties. Only the most sweeping vistas of territory in the nineteenth century, the most expansive Gross National Product in the twentieth, supported a popular confidence that all Americans could carve their monopolies from such a feast of opportunities. Otherwise, everybody's realm became nobody's land where competitors, scrambling to extend their boundaries as fast and as far as they could, at least laid claim to future rights—posted, keep out—if they could not immediately build their fences.

America was a complex map of circumscribed privileges. Liberty for one unit stretched to the point where another's began. Traditions, like rights, were almost always specific and contained: the heritage of the Concord town meeting, the history of Calhoun County, the special contribution of Italian-Americans, the unique professionalism of the law. To dissent from the ways of the segment meant in the end to evacuate, to create a new domain with its own rules and prerogatives. The communitarian impulse of the nineteenth century and its modifications in the twentieth simply extended this normal American pattern. From New Harmony to Pullman, from exurbia to the student communes, the appropriate means of following a different persuasion were secession and insulation. Occupational subspecialties detached themselves from larger subspecialties in that same search for distinctiveness, and they redefined homogeneity, demanded autonomy, and cultivated their own traditions in an effort to guarantee yet another boundary on the map. People who did not take the proper initiative were volunteered: an African colony for free blacks in the early nineteenth century, a vacant spot almost anywhere on the globe for Europe's Jews in the early 1940s.

Across these barriers Americans constructed a transactional society whose cohesion relied upon the general acceptance of a common game. Its origins antedated industrialism and transcended Calvinism, however compatible each was with American values. Its families raised children to take their places in a world of compartments where people negotiated only with equals or through intermediaries, where a broader fabric of relationships was construed either as contests or as contracts. The indispensable servants of this society were advocates and brokers—the lobbies and the legislature—who apportioned its privileges among otherwise separated groups, and its strength was the sum of these agreements. "Unless there is a deposit of values shared by interacting individuals," Robert Merton has stated, "there exist social relations . . . but no society." The deposit of values —the commitment to a common game—was remarkably strong, but by sharing values that inherently discouraged interaction, Americans seemed bent upon creating a society with a minimum of social relations.

Transactions were neither interactions nor a preparation for them. Whenever Americans were stripped of their rules and intermediaries, they found free interchange a disturbing time for awkwardly egalitarian probes, suspicion, retreat. After a prolonged stay abroad Henry James noted that quality almost as soon as he arrived in New York. Upon encountering a group of laborers, James immediately felt a "chill": "What lapsed, on the spot, was the element of communication with the workers, as I may call it for want of a better word; that element which in a European country, would have operated, from side to side, as the play of mutual recognition . . . and involving, for the moment, some impalpable exchange." During the 1930s, elites suffered as much distress from their feelings of social looseness as from the facts of social legislation. Similarly during the 1960s, an American malaise grew in proportion to the threat of unstructured relations—between blacks and whites, youth and adults, citizens and officials, women and men. Rules of transaction were being violated and realms of privacy invaded; let arbitrators settle the problems, deal only with the leaders, expel the disorderly students, pass a law, somehow reestablish the proper barriers and procedures. As in the 1880s and the 1930s, the employment of private policemen suddenly soared. Blacks exaggerated the significance of their color, just as radicals exaggerated the impact of their ideology, in the responses they drew. A few years later, these same dissenters—black or bearded or braless —received a passable welcome in elite segments, for now they came through proper channels as recruits rather than invaders. It had been the vision of obsolete codes and crumbling walls that had spread panic in the sixties far beyond the points of immediate encounter.

The one area sufficiently free from such anxieties to allow public experimentation was the segment itself. In a collection of equals, the agreement on certain fundamentals, the reserve of concern, and the continuity in traditions offered a standing possibility for the kinds of interaction and compromise that public behavior required. The richest opportunities lay in those communities integrating work, home, sexes, and age groups into a scheme that managed a full range of daily activities, and the history of house-raising and midwifery, cooperative harvesting and church socials illustrated its importance in an impressive variety of circumstances. By the twentieth century the parcelling of life into many functions restricted, although it certainly did not destroy that potential. As lives increasingly divided into categories of residence and occupation, women proved more adaptive than men. While suburban wives pooled resources for better schools, collaborative child care, and neighborhood improvement, women in small towns and urban enclaves were making the most imaginative efforts to retain traditional ways. Some qualities of mutuality also appeared as an informal supplement to occupational life. A crisis could expose pockets of a public tradition that employees or colleagues had scarcely noticed forming.

The total effect of these public traditions was not overwhelming. From the collapse of the original Jamestown settlement, to the disappearance of common fields in the middle colonies, to the immediate need in New England for legislation in place of custom, the bias of community life from the outset had favored private rights. Although there were significant realms of public behavior in the nineteenth-century community, the high incidence of mobility and the pressure for individual achievement were always attenuating them. Some subsections in the cities contained notable records of mutual help and cooperation, but as Sam Bass Warner, Jr., has demonstrated, they developed in an alien environment. Functional organization in the twentieth century gave no formal encouragement to public experimentation. Inside America's compartments, a public tradition endured without flourishing.

The very qualities sustaining this modest public tradition halted it at the compartmental boundaries. Concern, trust, loyalty turned inward in a segmented society. The successful community accentuated its members' sense of difference from all other groups. By definition, the units of specialization in the twentieth century rewarded members for the purity of their resolve to an occupation. Professionals were hired, paid, and honored for such priorities; corporate executives who worried about consumer rights, or doctors who pondered the illnesses of the poor, automatically raised questions about their dedication and dependability. A social university or a people's law firm, quite apart from the problems of implementation, was an inherent contradiction. America's answer to class consciousness, as to all broad social loyalties, was segmentation, a system of insular units each maximizing its power and rewards according to the counter-ideology of "More, now!" Unions that protected featherbedding and antiquated building codes, like Protestant denominations that guarded their sectarian identities, were merely fulfilling the charges of a larger society where issues extraneous to the compartment belonged either to the operations of a whole scheme, perhaps to the government officials assigned to care for them, but not to the ordinary citizen. Public in this wider sense connoted something out there, someone else's problems.

On grounds common to many people, Americans behaved according to this logic of otherness. They littered the parks and sidewalks and paid an escalating price to have them cleaned by somebody else. When a national gathering of Jehovah's Witnesses left Yankee Stadium spotless, commentators noted the peculiarities of a particular group, not the appropriate treatment of a public facility. Other groups might or might not exercise this private option. Cranks, solicitors, and casual, everyday rudeness defined the telephone outside its standardized uses as an amoral instrument. Sensible drivers learned to face the highways as random warfare among mechanized maniacs, and a sticker of the American flag was perfectly compatible with the car speeding through a school zone at noon. To the extent that people accepted the discipline of the queue, they did so for a payoff, to fulfill no more than a necessary transaction. After they had formed lines for a ticket, they trampled each other for a seat in the subway or theater. The decorum of the home simply had no relationship with the garbage in the gutter or the elbows at the store counter.

Within such a setting no sources existed to create a distinctive sense of public property. American values made the term itself a defensive one, for property carried a silent modifier "private" that dominated its conception and uses. Citizens in the nineteenth century treated public property as pre-private, as a preliminary and temporary condition that beckoned to the ambitious. From the public domain to the public printing contract, it was something to grab and hoard before another person could. Who would take it, not what would happen to it, generated the great debates. In the twentieth century, as government holdings expanded with its functions, public property increasingly acquired the characteristics of private property: a building or territory bounded by its own lines and protected from encroachment by its own code of limitations—another package of rights held apart. It also had owners and managers, officials whose proprietary attitudes excluded the possibility of any real public use. Unless public mirrored private property, nothing would save it from the normal, amoral abuses of a common facility.

Neutral meeting places were exceedingly rare in a society of parcelled domains. The common grounds of popular myth —the beaches and ball parks, the voting booths, the boot camps—offered scant opportunities for encounter and discovery. Usually lacking even such way stations as the pub, Americans relied upon the standard courtesy of bringing home a friend, a practice that forced a selection between private castles and presumed intimacy before exploration. The young had public schools, but the social values there discouraged much tentative give-and-take among different people. In the nineteenth century, the schools preached a simple set of absolutes, a universal extension of the model community. In the twentieth, they either buried differences in a synthetic American homogeneity or envisaged many peoples bringing many gifts to the nation, an antiseptic pluralism not unlike so many strangers depositing dimes in the contribution box. After 1940 a growing segregation by income and status reinforced the school's message of insularity. Without preparation for unusual encounters, Americans responded to the random mixing of diverse people as recent studies have indicated they should: they left more hardened in their antagonisms than they had come. Americans, like cats, felt their confidence drain as they moved farther from their base, whether it was a geographical or an occupational one. A visit to the center of an unfamiliar city communicated quite literally a sense of being nowhere—utterly vulnerable in a formless world. Little wonder that the attempts by radical youth in the 1960s to create public arenas—a people's park or a street dance or a sidewalk discussion—conjured visions of mess and threat, prospects of lawless little jungles filled with unknown dangers.

A sense of social responsibility, like the curve of confidence, dropped sharply beyond the borders of the segment. The deep American hostility to taxation, dating well before it united colonists during the 1760s and operating ever since to hold levels remarkably low in such a wealthy land, expressed more than an anal attachment to one's own money. The resistance almost always arose over kind rather than amount. Levies for a railroad promotion or a public school, just as informal tithes for the church or fees for the club, often made excellent sense in a local setting and brought generous returns with little resentment. Taxes for broader public purposes, on the other hand, seemed a raid on the righteous, funds spirited away for someone else's benefit. When an innovative program required a subsidy, it was usually told, in a cliché with devastating consequences for public policies, to meet the test of the marketplace.

Federal taxes were justifiable only if they appeared essential to the maintenance of a national system. Little in the nineteenth century qualified—for some a tariff, for most just a pittance to sustain the government. In the twentieth century it required the Great Depression to link continuing, expensive government services with the preservation of a system, and international crisis then added hugely to the foundation laid in the thirties. It was during this major departure that the income tax acquired its popular legitimacy. By midcentury, however, the hyperboles of system maintenance were accompanying almost every government program, for no other arguments would do, and in time the general blare of lies made almost all programs suspect. Promises to lower taxes, which had never lost their appeal, rose in popularity during the 1960s and 1970s. Although President Nixon might infuriate members of Congress by refusing to implement an anti-pollution law, he successfully muted popular criticism by identifying his decision with government economy. The residents of Santa Barbara might agonize over an oil slick and the residents of Searsport, Maine, might block the establishment of a new refinery, but nationally the dominant issue was the price of fuel—payoff, not high-priced public purpose.

To do your best inside the segment fulfilled all but the most exceptional requirements of citizenship. You did not discriminate against blacks, your local schools had integrated, your advertising firm welcomed good people of any color or sex. If your unit was an island of virtue, you had accomplished everything that a reasonable person could ask. It was a matter less of priorities than of sufficiency; wider juries, a broader accountability, scarcely existed. America revealed a good deal about its standards of social responsibility by the allocation of scarce resources. People who agreed that medical care should not depend upon income could still live comfortably in a suburb adjacent to Chicago with a doctor for each 200 residents, while the city's West Side provided one doctor for each 30,000. Who, beyond a disembodied system, was responsible—to whom and why? Those in the late 1960s whose only prescription for the nation was to turn itself around indicated quite understandably that they could not answer the question. Beneath a certain crudeness of phrasing, Dr. Morris Fishbein of the American Medical Association captured a basic truth about American society when he wrote in 1939: "A little sickness is not too great a price to pay for maintaining democracy in times like these."

By comparison with other modern nations, poverty in America was not severe. Although it belied each pretension to affluence for all, it did not constitute a unique condemnation of the American economy. What it primarily revealed was the ease with which a segmented people accepted inequalities. Comfortable Americans had to rediscover poverty every generation or so—the 1830s, the 1870s, the 1900s, the 1930s, the 1960s—because it was forever disappearing from sight. Sometimes they were encouraged to find it by a new conception of poverty's cause and cure; sometimes a major depression forced it into view. Yet if these discoveries did not come by chance, they recurred only because of a striking capacity to look without perceiving, to note without feeling. The heart of the matter was neither optimism nor hypocrisy; it was indifference.

The American way of redressing the human costs of inequality was charity, a tradition admirably suited to a segmented society. Individuals and small groups rather than distant powers made the decisions of when, how much, and to whom they gave. Even a small contribution brought feelings of virtue—a gift rather than an obligation, an aid to good conscience rather than a reminder of bad. In difficult times no particular guilt attached itself to a change of mind. As an official in the Department of Commerce explained in 1970 when corporations were ignoring their pledges to support black capitalism, "It's hard to imbue businessmen with social consciousness when business is bad." Above all, charity reinforced a scheme of transactions and payoffs. For the giver—to the deserving poor of the nineteenth century or the United Fund of the twentieth—it represented an informal contract by which the recipient, in exchange for a payoff, would remain sealed in another domain. Sharing with the less fortunate, a lesson comfortable Americans learned as soon as they were old enough to enter church and school, or buying an apple on the street corner in 1932, purchased a form of immunity from actual confrontation, and so in rough measure charity always did.

In the twentieth century, when government assumed responsibility for a large number of charity's customary realms, charity's transactional values came with them. As the payoffs became more specific and predictable, the concept of an insurance contract also grew more precise. Because peace was defined as the absence of conflict—a void—only complete insulation could achieve it, and signs that the recipients of public aid might still disturb other people's lives not only exposed the troublemakers as dishonorable but also eroded confidence in entire programs. What good was the WPA if the workers struck? The very presence of picketing welfare mothers marked the scheme a failure. An ideal of unawareness, of no feelings whatsoever, had prompted these public bargains, and the taxpayers demanded a proper return on their investment. In America, the contract itself was justice.

Although government management was asked increasingly to produce miracles of peace—eliminate discrimination or drugs or even unrest—the officials who implemented these programs did not rise accordingly in stature, as the popularity of the menial title "civil servant" indicated. Except for the most exalted positions of unity and maintenance—the President, the Supreme Court, the chief brokers in Congress, and a handful of others—the preface "public" to a job connoted at best a routine efficiency, more likely the boring cul de sac of bureaucracy. Public occupations, like other versions of the public in America, simply lacked substance. Officials were expected to be the invisible workers who filled the cracks of a segmented society, and they attracted widespread attention only when they failed, when trouble slipped through the walls. Private values tended to fill the vacancy of these public norms. Bargains for personal gain between policemen and criminals, or tax assessors and real estate investors, represented, in many instances, a merging of interests around the only available standard.

The poor reputation of government officials was one index to a particularly sharp liberal frustration in the twentieth century: the persistent elusiveness of a new and vital public consciousness. This liberal hope appeared early in the century along with the need to separate public from private spheres of responsibility. Before the twentieth century, a clear distinction between the two had not seemed essential. People as varied as Robert Morris, Roger Taney, and Rutherford Hayes had been encouraged to take high office on the assurance that their private pursuits would not suffer. The qualifications for public office in the eighteenth and nineteenth centuries had been a natural, fluid extension of private life, an extrapolation from a single, universally applicable core of character that guaranteed a basic integrity in everything the individual undertook. A truly good man could simultaneously follow his personal and official pursuits without endangering either. In a modern system of functions, however, public occupations required their own specific qualities just as each category of life did. Yet unlike civil engineering or paper manufacturing, the strength of public occupations in a democracy would depend ultimately upon a widespread sense among its citizens of clear public purposes. Because liberals found no basis for such a public consciousness in their compartmentalized nation, they sought it above or apart from its selfish units. America would require an enlightened, dedicated cadre to create what these reformers thought Britain or Germany enjoyed as a birthright—a natural consequence of social traditions. The central agent in this progressive conception was the public man, a model of impartial wisdom, who stood free from society's parts so that he could speak and act for an entire nation. Soon this model would spread. The same characteristics would come to prevail in the government bureaus and commissions overseeing critical areas of the modern economy, and, in appropriate degree, among lesser officials as well: at each level of government, involved yet detached, political yet scientific.

From progressivism to the New Deal to the New Frontier, successive generations of liberal reformers and their theorists —Herbert Croly in the 1900s, E. Pendleton Herring in the 1930s, Grant McConnell in the 1960s—offered variations of this hope in their visions of a better social order. Originally, the public ideal emphasized a state of mind, one associated in particular with the discipline of scientific expertise. By the 1930s, liberals were concentrating quite specifically upon Washington. Through careful planning and implementation, the national government would build a public sector and a public consciousness would grow with the new sphere. The revival of the 1960s, with its final burst in Eugene McCarthy's campaign of 1968, stressed goals, clear points of attraction that would draw citizens from their narrow lives and mobilize their energies behind broad national objectives. The proliferation of national commissions to define these goals served, along with the popularity of the Kennedys, as the primary expression of this latest yearning for a vital public purpose.

Each of these visions faded. The twenties proclaimed the superiority of business leadership, the fifties glorified the effects of a benign pluralism, and the early seventies declared the sovereignty of a silent majority; but none of these could satisfy the urge for a transcendent public sphere, a realm of commonality that surmounted segmentation. In its place Americans drew what comfort they could from certain traditional assumptions about the sources of social reform. Recent ecological causes illustrated one of these, the multiplication of atomized private acts. If each individual used only biodegradable products, shunned items with animal fur, composted organic materials, bought solely from ethical companies, and so on, the combination of such acts with the particles contributed by many, many others would ultimately pile into a public solution. It was the same kind of public that opinion polls or voting offered: millions of private decisions privately executed would create public policy. At least one set of individuals collecting the litter that another had strewn would keep the trash from accumulating.

A second tradition relied upon the workings of an invisible hand. The most popular version invested its faith in an expanding GNP, a focus of attention that was already a primary source of American cohesion. Assuming that the social system was basically sound, greater national wealth should automatically diminish all problems and dissolve most. Here was modern America's homeopathic cure: problems in a system of payoffs would be solved by more payoff. Although some of these expectations also involved a smoother and more efficient central management, private mechanisms gained favor in times of disillusionment over a public consciousness. The appearance around 1970 of a great many plans to open such areas as education, the mail, and city services to a freer play of the private market belonged to a pattern of revivals that had also occurred in the 1920s and 1950s. What identified the traditions of an atomized citizenry and an invisible hand as American was their common assumption that public results did not require public processes, that collective ends need not violate insular procedures. By the tests of human interaction and accommodation, the public was bankrupt in modern America.

Public action, along with all aspects of American society, was significantly affected in the twentieth century by the rising importance of power values—that is, values justifying control over other people's behavior. From the beginning, power as local autonomy had been basic to a segmented society, and the vigil against alien impingements had appeared as soon as Americans organized their communities. For more than a century after the Revolution, any leader who represented several insular units had promised as a matter of course to protect their compartmental sovereignty. The dearness of broad social power had made it a slyly coveted commodity, and throughout the nineteenth century, the desire for a sweeping authority had reappeared as the occasional surfacing of a subterranean envy. The obsession with vast conspiratorial networks, the vision of evangelizing the nation or the world, the glorification of command on the battlefield, the respect for entrepreneurs who overrode all obstacles to seize economic empires, all had expressed such covert desires. But the moral resolution in each of these instances—the crusade against subversives, the voluntarism of religious conversion, the abnormality of war, the condemnation of corporate monopoly—had formally repudiated the coercion of others. Legitimate power could come only as a consequence of intrinsic merit: the irresistibility of a truth, the emulation of a moral model, the economic results of a virtuous life. It would always preserve individual freedom and, above all, compartmental autonomy.

These direct, uncomplicated lines from character to achievement belonged on the parallel tracks of nineteenth-century America. In the far tighter society of the twentieth century, the techniques of resolving problems among these jealous, interdependent units transformed both the meaning and the significance of power. Modern managerial leadership meant the conscious manipulation of people for social purposes. Manipulation, in other words, was power—the ability to arrange and persuade, entice and intimidate—and the more challenging the tasks of leadership, the greater the manipulative range they required. Once it had become intimately associated with leadership, power entered generally into the measures of elite prestige. It affected the status of groups as different as entertainers, who could play the emotions of millions through mass media, and scientists, whose findings might reshape the world. It identified such new professions as advertising and public relations as particularly desirable occupations, and it endowed such old categories as college teachers, who molded each generation of leaders, and judges, who dictated the meaning of the law, with a fresh importance. In time elites could openly boast about the artificial markets they had created in order to receive new products, and the voters they had herded behind candidates. In time also Robert McNamara could leave Ford Motors, and with it most of his salary and privacy, to gain new stature as Secretary of Defense, an awesome domain for manipulation. Even the jargon of ordinary elite life—one upsmanship, the games people play—reflected an understanding of everyday human relations as so many maneuvers for an incremental domination of others.

One of the goals of elite manipulation was to convince other Americans that the old virtues still prevailed, that an isolated individual achievement remained the only honorable source of success. But as early as the 1920s the primary objects of manipulation were also expressing their attachment to power values, usually through fantasies of invulnerability to any outside influences. They applauded Charlie Chaplin's elusive, insouciant little tramp, cheered Hollywood's omnicompetent heroes and brutally independent antiheroes, and followed the exploits of their favorite supermen in the comic strips. Long before automobile manufacturers finally responded with appropriate styles and names—Cougar, Sabre, Mustang—anonymous owners were tinkering with engines, dragging the highways, and challenging any passerby with the American's most available instrument of personal power.

A new sensitivity to power helped to reshape American attitudes toward routine work. During the era of character and achievement, work had been expected to carry its own rewards. Dedication had demonstrated character, and in a proper world, character would eventually bring its returns. In the modern scale of occupations, the importance of work derived almost exclusively from the nature of the job, not the nature of the worker. Well past mid-century certain members of the elite could still declare their allegiance to the traditional values of character and achievement because to people with positions of high prestige, the new extrinsic standards and the old intrinsic satisfactions might, in effect, coincide. But losers in the modern scheme knew better. Where the judgment of the nineteenth century had told Americans to hate themselves when they failed, its counterpart in the twentieth told Americans to hate their jobs when they failed. Power became an increasingly critical component in that battle against failure. More and more conflicts between employers and employees were rooted in a struggle over shop controls, until by the 1970s every successful experiment in worker morale required greater autonomy on the job. Around 1930, the Hawthorne tests had indicated that human recognition would increase labor productivity. Now only power would suffice.

Although most Americans were not peculiarly powerless by any normal comparative standard, their society made them feel that way and feel a grinding frustration because of it. The consequences appeared everywhere during the 1960s. Experts established those feelings as the primary cause of the nation's great addiction, alcoholism. Certain scholars declared that a system of corporate power lay behind every significant decision, foreign and domestic, in this century. Black Power captured the civil rights movement, and opponents countered with mimicking slogans of White Power, Polish Power, Southern Power. Leaders in the woman's movement located power as the crux of their oppression and the lever for their emancipation. In France, Simone de Beauvoir had developed a complex analysis of woman's interior, social, and philosophical identity; in America, Kate Millett provided instead a simple, pointed exposition of male power. Militant students adopted the same approach in their attacks on tyranny at home and in school. Power dominated the idiom of dissent only because its values had come to pervade a whole society. By the 1960s it was the natural American perception of human relations.

The popularization of power values unquestionably complicated the problems of management in a segmented society. Almost any variation on the rationale of character and achievement suited a nation of compartments far better than the need for power. Because achievement required only a yardstick, it allowed people to function in separate spheres, competitive at a distance, even indifferent to one another. Power, on the other hand, demanded some form of interplay in order to determine dominance and subordinance. It encouraged overt rather than implicit social contests, and it certainly did nothing to discourage open conflict. When the style of leaders became everyone's style, the elite model of modern society worked only under continuing stress. In addition, power values gave exploratory interactions precisely the qualities most detrimental to the development of a public realm. If encounters were confrontations, the chances for mutual adjustments and equal access diminished sharply. The pressure to win, the assumption that one group's gain anywhere along a common border could only mean another group's loss, removed in many instances the last potential for public experimentation. From the battles over public schools and universities to the collapse of an interracial civil rights movement and the Office of Economic Opportunity, the late sixties and early seventies wrote a monotonous story of the failure of such tentative explorations. Meanwhile, by helping to define the meaning of international relations, these same power values were also exercising a profound influence on America's behavior in the world at large.

America never seemed to have the leeway or space for public purposes. In world affairs, on the other hand, it appeared to have endless options in a vast arena. This vacuous international setting had two entwined consequences that were formative in America's foreign relations. First, for most Americans during most of American history, it gave that wider world a quality of fundamental irrelevance, an unrelatedness to normal life that conditioned outlooks as much in war as it did in peace and influenced aggressive foreign policies as much as it did cautious ones. As late as the 1950s, a national poll revealed that more than four out of five Americans had never discussed their attitudes on foreign policy with a friend, let alone taken action on them, and beneath this silence lay the even more crucial assumption that in a proper dispensation Americans should never need to discuss such matters. Second, the responsibility for dealing with this presumably irrelevant world fell into a very few hands, notably those of the federal executive. In only slightly simplified terms, foreign affairs belonged to the President.

An almost atmospheric security sustained this American sense of distance from the rest of the world. Even in the era of the Revolution, when Americans of all types expressed their deep involvement with European events, a quality of apartness was modifying that concern, not so much to weaken it as to suggest a country of spectators rather than participants, a way of thinking rather than a cause for action. America was certainly not a free international agent nor would it approximate one for decades to come. Decisions made in Europe prepared the route to Revolution, allowed it to succeed, and continued to buffer the nation well past the War of 1812. Yet whatever the sources, the effect was a remarkable freedom. Moreover, during the long process of industrial development, the United States retained an impressive degree of economic autonomy—a reserve capacity to function reasonably well on its own resources. Until the mid-twentieth century an international economy affected America's rate of growth without dictating its survival as a modern nation. Although the meaning of apartness had basically changed by the 1950s, a heritage at least two centuries old altered very slowly, very grudgingly.

"Man for the most part conceives of what is remote, unknown, or difficult to understand in terms of what is near, well known, and self-evident," Ernst Topitsch has reminded us. In America this principle acquired a striking simplicity. A minimum of dependence on the world abroad, a minimum of impingement from that world on everyday life, meant a minimum of adjustment to it as a special sphere with rules and a reality of its own. From any domestic point of departure—a community, a region, an occupational unit, a nation— an American method of understanding could extend outward without encountering barriers that demanded reconsideration. Although Americans behaved in many ways like European imperialists as they moved across the continent, they still were not required to reconceive that behavior, to calculate new territory and strange people by standards other than the ones they ordinarily used. In a compartmentalized society, aliens had always appeared very quickly along any map. As Americans projected their view beyond the national boundaries, they simply did not shift their basis for understanding. No fault line divided the world into qualitatively distinct categories, one with national and the other with extranational characteristics. Even those members of a twentieth-century elite who considered the nation as a critical line of defense expressed the same kinds of anxieties about domestic and foreign enemies, as their persistent, indiscriminate blending of the two demonstrated. With only minor variations Americans applied the logic of segmentation universally.

This framework made it possible to recognize how certain charges commonly leveled against Americans were simultaneously illuminating and misleading. By European standards, Americans were indeed provincial, undisciplined, and irresponsible in foreign affairs. Because so little mediated between their daily lives and the world at large, they could assume that their values applied everywhere, and therefore they were provincial. Because no steady, abrasive interaction had forced them to learn accommodation, they could approach international problems with a quality of abandon—sometimes casual, sometimes reckless—and therefore they were undisciplined. Because necessity did not hold them to a fixed course in foreign affairs, they could make unpredictable shifts without suffering abnormal losses, and therefore they were irresponsible. But European standards did not fit the American experience. What might have been immaturity or arrogance in a European setting was a reasonable consequence of insularity and compartmentalization, a rational extension of American interests as Americans could understand them.

International security and domestic segmentation combined to concentrate the responsibility for foreign affairs inside a very small circle of leaders. On the issue of a monopoly by insiders, the most conservative and the most radical diplomatic historians agreed, even as they debated fiercely which tiny group had done what and why. Public discussion rarely affected either the content or the process of international decisions, and leaders who expressed an interest in popular sentiment on such matters were usually fulfilling a democratic ritual. Because so few made these decisions with so little outside scrutiny, they always remained vulnerable to charges of intrigue and deceit. But instead of a series of plots, it was a broad traditional acceptance that established the conditions of leadership in foreign affairs and generally endorsed its conduct.

The origins of this special privilege lay in the hierarchical society of the eighteenth century. The citizens of a town or county expected the very top of their social pyramid to deal with the outside world in their behalf. For a local group, that involved relations with neighboring settlements, at most a colony or state. However, the government of that colony or state also constituted a pyramid, and its hierarchy, in turn, elevated from the collection of local leaders a very few to meet its outside world. This process, repeated among the delegates from many colonies or states, meant that an exceptionally refined elite of the elites negotiated with the powers abroad. It was a responsibility bearing the mark of highest distinction, a judgment that certain men were equal to any public task, and by the same reasoning, their failure in that wider world would disqualify them for the most exalted positions of domestic leadership. Foreign and domestic issues were, in fact, merged in the eighteenth century. Because feelings of attachment followed the dictates of belief and family ties rather than geography, distant events could have an intensely personal meaning for ordinary citizens, as their passionate loyalties to Britain and France during the 1790s illustrated, and they responded in waves of approval and anger to their leaders' decisions on foreign policy. Both the immanence and importance of this international framework were expressed in the Constitutional title, Secretary of State, which only in retrospect seemed a curious designation for diplomatic responsibilities.

The Constitution limited the management of foreign affairs to this winnowed elite: the President, his closest advisers, and the Senate. Appropriately, it was assumed that the Secretary of State was serving as the President's heir-apparent, a tradition that with one exception and minor variations held until 1828. It lasted so long only because the special significance and skills associated with international problems continued to support traditional ways in national government even as eighteenth-century society was disintegrating at the local and state levels. But no Secretary of State after John Quincy Adams apprenticed naturally for the Presidency. As Americans pushed relentlessly along their parallel tracks, an outside world, whose distance was now comprehended in miles as well as ideas, rapidly receded. Except on issues of North American expansion, where everyone was an expert, foreign affairs belonged to the very few who cared, or whose offices required them to care. As one might have assigned Sanskrit to the scholar with a certain awe but little interest, so foreign affairs, with an occasional, noisy exception, were delegated to a handful of officials, then largely forgotten.

As an esoteric field, it set apart the scattering of men who studied it. Although Charles Sumner's senatorial colleagues generally ignored him on domestic affairs, they listened respectfully to his elaborate abstractions on international matters. The effects of that tradition remained as late as the First World War, when Henry Cabot Lodge and Elihu Root, politically weak on most domestic issues, always commanded attention for their peculiar knowledge of international subjects. Above all, however, prerogative in foreign affairs belonged to the President, a specialist only by the obligations of his office, whose primary task was to manage these matters so that they did not disturb other Americans. For mistakes here more than in any other area, Presidents were held personally responsible, and on questions involving a major power, whatever fiery statements they might issue, they acted very cautiously. They understood that the ideal administration of foreign affairs would leave most Americans unaware that there were any foreign affairs. A sphere that had been bestowed upon the Presidents of the eighteenth century because of its high importance remained theirs in the nineteenth because of its slight consequence.

From that legacy Presidents in the twentieth century were able to construct a grand bastion of power. The elite rationale for segmentation was the right of those with unique skills to control various areas of specialization in behalf of the general welfare, and government officials used that same reasoning to justify their autonomy in the many realms they came to manage. Departments and bureaus and commissions argued that only they, and perhaps the private groups they supervised, had the data, knowledge, and dedication to make intelligent decisions, much as doctors and chemists did in their areas. Unlike doctors and chemists, however, most government officials felt the need to report periodically on their stewardship, to renew their claims to autonomy through simplified explanations of their complicated operations. Thus citizens were asked to appraise a national budget according to the principles of a household budget, but they were told to accept the executive's management of it because its tangle of technicalities far exceeded their understanding.

Although the planned obsolescence of citizenship had uneven results in the many areas where it was attempted, it did work very effectively in foreign affairs. More and more small groups, usually business interests, demanded a place in international policymaking, but the overwhelming majority of

Americans retained the traditional assumption that in a correctly ordered society they should not have to be bothered by the world. A brief peak of involvement around the First World War was followed by the normal trough of unconcern, reasonably summarized as the isolationism of the 1920s and 1930s. Thus the Second World War appeared as yet another appalling aberration, and the problems of the Cold War as a sequence of infuriating intrusions by an evil, alien imperialism. When divisions of the national government expanded enormously to meet these issues, their operations were far better sealed from public criticism than any other area of the bureaucracy. International finance, for example, was not intrinsically more complex than national finance, but by prior definition the one fell outside and the other inside the bounds of relevance.

With a ring of specialized agencies surrounding him, the President managed this realm in exceptional freedom. Only the most calamitous prospects such as wars required serious public discussion, and even these decisions, once made, quickly fell within the President's discretion. Rallying loyally and mindlessly behind a leader in wartime just because it was wartime had no clear precedent from previous centuries; it involved a peculiarly modern application of expert rule in an area where only one expert prevailed and where everyone else's stake was simply the disappearance of an abnormal disruption. As in the case of domestic policies, the President and his advisers from time to time felt obliged to report to the public, but in foreign affairs the simplifications were more self-consciously elementary, verging, in fact, upon a ritual of slogans that both speaker and listener could recognize as such: clean out those rats in Berlin, win the Four Freedoms, stop Communist aggression. As "Dr. New Deal," Roosevelt devised simple explanatory models in order to persuade and recruit, to mobilize political support. As "Dr. Win-the-War," he employed homey analogies to calm and inspire, to improve national morale. During the thirties he maneuvered and listened and responded; during the forties he retired to deal with the world. The impeccably liberal Adlai Stevenson could declare in one breath that "our political institutions have matured around the idea of popular consent as the only valid basis of government and of political power," and argue with the next that in the face of an extraordinarily complex "Communist conspiracy" the President should immunize himself from "the public appetite for simple solutions" and follow his own special, sophisticated knowledge. In the context of this American tradition, one can appreciate Lyndon Johnson's conduct of the Indochinese War—the secretiveness, the soothing public statements, the search for a quick, clear solution. It was the President's problem, just as it was the President's right to determine both strategy and tactics. The public could only demand results.

In an uncertain contemporary world the risks for a President ran high, as Johnson discovered by 1968. After all, it *was* Johnson's war, just as earlier ones with some justice had been identified with Madison, Polk, Wilson, and Franklin Roosevelt. To require domestic insulation from the effects of international affairs, to punish a President when an intruding messiness passed the low levels of public tolerance, placed every modern President at the edge of failure. Yet the few attempts to alter this system of responsibility accomplished nothing. Talk about a national referendum on war continued as Truman was sending troops to Korea. Senator J. William Fulbright's call for greater congressional powers drew a scattering of applause while Johnson and Nixon were selecting the places and means for war in Asia. Instead, Americans demanded new leaders for old, fresh competence at the helm when an old commander lost control. Not even a political party could expect much credit or blame. Eisenhower—not the Republican party—would end that troublesome war which Truman could not stop. So, as Johnson's successor, would Nixon. And the rewards came as high as the risks. Memories of Truman as a tough defender of his nation in crisis gave him an otherwise unattainable reputation. Nothing more authoritatively established John Kennedy as a leader than his encounter with the Soviet Union over missiles in Cuba. With the confrontation past before Americans knew it had occurred, no one was disturbed and only success followed: perfect management. Just as dramatically, Nixon traveled half a globe to stabilize relations with China, and Americans could watch him do it in the security of their living rooms. Again, it was the epitome of what Americans asked of their President in foreign affairs, what they would repay at the polls.

For good reasons of prudence and pride, Presidents had long taken their responsibility in foreign affairs very seriously. However solicitous some of them were to this or that private group, they guarded their right to establish priorities and fix objectives with a determination that at times seemed obsessive. A Grant or McKinley or Eisenhower, who proved so mild before Congress on domestic issues, could stand like a Spartan in the pass protecting his privileges on international matters. How a President behaved in foreign affairs, therefore, told far less about a configuration of special interests manipulating him than it did about the qualities he, just as any citizen, drew from his society. No separate tradition shaped assumptions or trained leaders for international relations, and Presidents, like other Americans, used whatever lay at hand to understand them.

Americans required a sense of boundaries in the wider world, lines that would separate the acceptable from the unacceptable. By whatever standards prevailed in their segments, they divided the globe with as much precision as they could; and they construed those inside the limits as somehow essentially like themselves—democratic nations, Nordic peoples, a Free World—and those beyond as fundamentally different—autocratic, racially inferior, Communist. Although international alliances were tense and tentative, as they would be with any distant segment, the American camp still had to approximate the ideal of homogeneity. The most generous view of events inside these boundaries interpreted them as movements toward an American norm: the Revolutions of 1848 as a step toward American democracy, the formulations of international law early in the 1900s as the preliminaries to an American Constitution for the civilized world, Israel as the story of another pioneering nation, plowing its desert as it replaced a variant of the Indians. Changes in world affairs brought changes in particular judgments, not in conceptions. Over the decades, Britain, France, Russia, Japan, Germany moved in and out of the acceptable realm without touching a major premise. The same distinctions applied to abrupt shifts in general outlook, such as the gyrations from horror to hope to bitterness accompanying the First World War. A sphere rapidly expanding or contracting was nevertheless a sphere. Neutral was an uncongenial term, usually connoting a kind of enmity, and when circumstances finally demanded an acknowledgment that many nations were following their own persuasions, another omnivorous category—the Third World—was required to make them comprehensible.

Not only was the world separated between friends and foes, but the choice of an approach to that world also tended to appear as a simple dichotomy: America as an isolated patch of liberty or America as a guide for all peoples, imperialism or anti-imperialism, make the world safe for democracy or return to normalcy, Fortress America or One World. Dangers arrived not in gradations but suddenly, whole. The compartmental wall, like virtue, was either there or not there, and solutions carried the same absolute meaning: either total victory or defeat. For those who understood peace as the absence of conflict, the strains of international life, particularly in the twentieth century, sent ominous signals. In retrospect, there had never been a real European peace between 1918 and 1939. The appropriate American label for the ambiguities of stress after 1945 was war—a Cold War—for they certainly did not register peace, and from the mid-fifties to the early seventies, Americans searched earnestly for the crucial moment when conditions had slipped across the magical line and ended that war.

With so little information and so many suspicions, Americans naturally found conspiracies a particularly congenial explanation for international behavior. A few of these conspiracies functioned exclusively abroad—a secret pact between Germany and Bolshevik Russia, for instance, in the final months of the First World War—but almost all in varying degrees involved domestic agents. Schemes to subvert the new nation, to detach its western territories, to manipulate international finance, to Bolshevize or Communize Amercia, all had run from abroad to officials, even neighbors at home. Other conspiracies had only an American cast. Because the conduct of foreign affairs always encouraged thoughts of a plot, some form of power elite could materialize on call: a Virginia clique, Polk and the slavocrats, Wilson's Anglophiles, Communists in government, the generals. People of all temperaments and styles joined in the search; Hubert Humphrey and Joseph McCarthy both operated in the 1950s from the premise of an international Communist conspiracy. Once again, the leeway for intrigue, the cover of secrecy, made a good deal of this analysis plausible. Did Franklin Roosevelt maneuver the United States into war or did he not?

This manner of understanding accentuated an American tendency to find meaning through abstractions. Masses of behavior that would otherwise have communicated only confusion were mastered by concepts: the evaluation of Europe in the eighteenth century by a republican model, continental dominion as manifest destiny in the nineteenth, the geopolitical fancies of Theodore Roosevelt's circle before the First

World War, and the disembodied reality of totalitarianism and communism around the Second World War. Even the mundane values of everyday experience produced a similar effect when they were projected across the world. Construing nations as personalities, treaties as handshakes, or wars as back alley brawls lifted the complexity of international events to an equally rarefied level of simple truths. These explanatory devises reinforced as they expressed the hard lines and clear patterns of a segmented cast of mind.

The American equation of law with order made legal abstractions a particularly valuable means of formulating world problems. Nothing offered greater comfort than the impression of an overarching pattern of natural or international law —some analogue to the Constitutional cover—governing all people, and documents that seemed to institutionalize this fundamental law, such as the Covenant of the League and the Charter of the United Nations, roused in certain Americans an almost messianic hope. But in a world of dubious members it was hard law—the law which drew lines and detailed procedures—that enjoyed a steady, broad popularity. At least as images, a code of neutral rights, a court of arbitration, a tribunal for war criminals suggested precisely the kind of impartial exactness promising to control the dangerously loose practices of international society. A sufficiently firm structure could police the globe. The limits of jurisdiction were in theory quite exact. As the protectors of compartmentalization, these mechanisms only maintained boundaries and regulated procedures, never tampered with a nation's—a segment's—internal affairs. Hints of a threat here, in fact, kept Americans skeptical about almost all the forms such proposals actually took.

The uses of these guidelines were legion. No accusation was more damning than the charge of international lawlessness, as Germany in particular discovered during the First World War, and officials solemnly juggled precedents in order to prove that every American action—the establishment of the Canal Zone, for instance, or the invasion of Mexico in 1916—was indeed a legal one. Where rules were lacking, Americans devised them. After the middle of the nineteenth century, each corollary to the Monroe Doctrine arrived as a new judicial pronouncement. One by one the modern wars added to the definition of a legal militarism. By the late 1960s fine distinctions between dirty and clean warfare—who was killed how by whom: soldier or civilian, man or woman, bombs or napalm, the line of battle or My Lai—could condone or condemn a particular slaughter in Indochina, and early in 1973 the question of legality, not lives, framed public debates over the massive bombing of Cambodia. As the record of the United States in Latin America illustrated, eligibility even to enter a system of rules depended upon a country's domestic compliance with a minimum American standard. By the same token, a skeletal structure of elections, courts, and a constitution, regardless of the substance around it, often qualified a nation as civilized. A test through legal forms served as an invaluable shorthand for sorting nations in categories of merit that both justified and influenced America's relations with them.

One cardinal principle of procedure in a segmented system was the necessity of negotiating solely through leaders. Brokerage and payoff required this specificity so that the contracts could be made and fulfilled through predictable channels. Despite an undercurrent of hope that appeals to a good citizenry might nullify the actions of a bad leader, Americans usually responded with disdain or confusion when the focus of responsibility in another nation was blurred. Why not war with Mexico in 1846 when no one could find its leaders? The coalitions and rotating premiers representing France and Italy after the Second World War eroded confidence in their capacity for any reliable transaction. The thought of dealing with whole bands of guerrillas or colonial peoples simply exceeded an American imagination. Intercepting dangerous international issues a safe distance from their lives was an important part of the protection that Americans demanded from their leaders, and the prospect of various heads of state resolving the big problems in a few hard hours of bargaining raised almost utopian hopes. Beginning with the Second World War, a great many Americans expected each meeting of the powerful managers to stabilize a chaotic world, and just as regularly they felt betrayed when basic conflicts rode right through the conferences at the summit.

Until the 1950s the sum of these characteristics was no more than an American approach to foreign affairs, in Dexter Perkins' phrase, an orientation from everyday life that experiences with the wider world had scarcely modified. Predilections were not policies, and the American record before the 1950s displayed little of the consistency, the continuity in design and execution, that qualified as policy. Despite the assumption after 1900 that the executive should in some sense act systematically, Presidents rarely brought their plans with them to office. Nor, as Wilson and Franklin Roosevelt demonstrated, did a new President feel obliged to complete the tasks of his predecessor, especially if the two represented different parties. As administrations came and went, no secure body of specialists remained at hand to smooth the transitions, to link the behavior of one with the next. Each President selected advisers by his own private standards, and the handful of experts who did persevere in the State Department during the first half of the twentieth century might or might not have access to the particular group now making the decisions. Most important, a high degree of unpredictability in resources—the need to mobilize power again and again in a society that granted these so sparingly for ventures abroad—inclined Presidents to abandon old programs and discouraged them from undertaking many new ones. Consequently, foreign affairs expressed an American logic without developing an American policy.

The nation's erratic imperial course illustrated these qualities. Treating all contiguous territories as somehow strategic and welcoming most opportunities to acquire them, Americans pushed fitfully westward under the cover of whatever rhetoric was appropriate to contemporary values. In the nineteenth century the crucial connection between parallel growth and space made additional land a passion, but what Americans craved had become theirs through the chances of European diplomacy and the softness of local resistance, not through the common objectives and strategies of successive administrations. Toward the end of the century, as the leeway within the United States seemed to disappear, territory overseas was one reasonable outlet. America could then compete with the other imperial powers along its own territorial channel. McKinley's decision to take the Philippines, in other words, was no aberration. But it still occurred through a fortuitous sequence of events rather than a President's design.

American imperialism grew more complex but not more predictable in the twentieth century. As more and more businessmen established long-term goals abroad—almost all of them dependent upon the government's assistance and almost none integrated with the others—their interests etched a busy network of international involvements that far exceeded the commitments any administration would undertake. Support was offered, then witheld, then offered again not in random fashion but with a sufficient responsiveness to Presidential bias, party affiliation, and particular friendships to give economic expansion a notably jerky, contingent quality. The government and various ambitious businessmen, while not necessarily at odds, simply operated under very different constraints, and the general absence of effective coalitions among these business interests—their reliance on a segmented style—further increased the likelihood of so many stops and starts. Only in Latin America did enough ends and means mesh over the years to fix a well-defined policy, a steady American resistance to any other nation's political or economic penetration. By the standards set in Europe, American imperialism was not peculiarly virulent. All the elements were there—the inhumanity, the pressure on weaker governments, the military interventions, the extraction of wealth—but the continuous application of national resources, the persistent use of a standing force which might have maximized their effect was missing.

Under these circumstances it made little sense before the 1950s to test America's foreign affairs against somebody's ideal of a true national interest. American society produced innumerable calculations and recalculations by the executive and a multiplicity of expansive private interests. In an American dispensation, each was as justifiable as the next, and the total of them represented the natural manner in which a segmented society dealt with the world. Similarly, no national standard measured different people's preferences in international matters. Hamilton's connivance with the British and Jefferson's with the French were equally appropriate in the United States of the 1790s; so in the nineteenth century were the loyalty of the Boston Irish to their homeland and the Boston patrician's attachment to England. Theodore Roosevelt was no more, no less American than Robert La Follette or Eugene Debs during the First World War. Some opinions carried more weight than others, but none more legitimacy. The sovereignty of each choice, the normlessness of a national context in which it was made, was a reflection of the singularly American and exclusively domestic sources for such preferences.

By the 1950s, America's relations with the world had changed in two fundamental respects. First, in an era of rockets and nuclear weapons, the nation was now uniquely vulnerable. Second, the executive had continuing access to the most formidable military resources in the world's history. From that new base the government devised a global policy called containment to limit the influence of Communist nations and their ideologies, negotiated an array of treaties to implement this policy, and deployed military resources to enforce it. Much that was customary passed into the new system. Containment itself was a model of American logic. It drew a line between friends and enemies, it exhorted citizens to perfect their internal homogeneity, and it promised the isolation, perhaps the extermination of an alien evil. At one level, it spun the grandest abstractions. At another, its treaties and informal bargains adapted America's transactional values to an international pattern of contracts and payoffs. In large measure because containment suited an American tradition so smoothly, it was a truly popular policy. Although the sheer quantity and spread of troubles attending it caused bursts of frustration, the policy itself remained remarkably free from criticism. Probably no other could have appealed so broadly. At the same time, Americans came to rely even more heavily upon Presidential management. Most of them continued to regard problems in Korea or Lebanon or Laos as essentially irrelevant to their lives, and they continued to judge a successful response by its capacity to insulate them from the repercussions. The decline of domestic turmoil over Indochina was itself proof of Nixon's superior handling of the war; the return of the last POW symbolically terminated that war.

Interwoven with these continuities, however, were profound changes at home and abroad. One of these fused world affairs with the basic scheme of American payoffs. Although the ties between these rewards and an international economy had gradually grown more extensive during the twentieth century, the critical shift came largely from domestic sources in a few pivotal years around midcentury. The investments of a hastily devised containment policy, not an evolving international dependence, joined world commitments and a system of payoffs on what appeared to be a permanent basis. The stabilizing capitalization of many major industries and the incentives for technological innovation—in other words, a fundamental part of the modern government's underwriting function—had become intimately bound to the nation's military program. Once wars had been the disrupters of payoff; now a demilitarized peace jeopardized it far more. Because reconsideration of the payoff system always threatened political disaster, something like a containment policy operated with a powerful self-generating force in contemporary America.

Power values accompanied America's managerial leadership in international affairs. Nothing exploded more dramatically in the discussions of the 1940s than the revelation that throughout its history, and particularly in the twentieth century, the crippling American weakness in world affairs had been an innocence about power. Only power—the capacity to counter, coerce, control, even obliterate—had international currency, and the lesson that could have avoided a Second World War would now be used to meet yet another amoral bloc of nations, the Communists. This orientation spread to influence the full content of American policy. As a self-evident proposition, it justified an escalating military budget. As a popular ethos, it glorified the manipulative wizardry of espionage. As a damning counter-argument, it eliminated the traditional tests that had once distinguished liberal nations as friends and reactionary ones as foes. As a new rule of the house, it encouraged the mentality of the game board, where countries were tokens, dominoes, to be won or lost in the abstract contests of force and pressure and hypothesized nuclear encounter that were now known as realism. Policy in world affairs required a new concern for priorities—what had precedence, where did a program fit, how would other purposes be affected in a total scheme of things—and the rationale of power increasingly predominated in these choices.

By placing foreign affairs in a discreet category, Americans gave free play to the effect of these values abroad. Few of the restraints that continued to hedge a President's options at home also applied to his actions in a wider world, where his rights—indeed his responsibilities—authorized whatever was necessary to insulate the nation. A vast arsenal of resources for use there seemed not merely safe because it would never endanger domestic arrangements but eminently wise because it would protect them. Only a general anxiety that he might have miscalculated, that certain measures were raising the risks of penetration from the outside, set a vague outer boundary on the executive's behavior, particularly in dealing with another thermonuclear power—the Soviet Union. Yet the President was the expert. Who could tell the doctor how best to treat the disease? Late in the sixties it required very concrete evidence immediately at hand—the draft, the flow of dour news from Saigon, the mass marches, the casualty lists, the most outrageous executive lies—to challenge the one person with the information and authority to manage this special realm.

Otherwise the principles of a segmented society applied with stark clarity across these distance areas. The striking limits of empathy spread a dehumanizing haze over the multitudes of the world where the devastation of a strange society—in Biafra, on the Plain of Jars—might elicit feelings similar to those for the extermination of whales. Peace as a void demanded their exclusion from American life, for interaction and accommodation would inevitably entail abrasions, eruptions, trouble. The values of power justified almost any manipulation involving almost any number of humans that would minimize disturbances from an alien source, and by the logic of those values, outsiders who did not respond to the subtler manipulations exposed themselves to a chilling sequence of more direct techniques for control. On a global scale, these issues placed domestic ones in proportion. A dissenter suppressed? Dictators installed. Violence in the streets? The destruction of nations. Discrimination against minorities? The brutalization of entire societies. The appalling price of an American system was paid abroad.

Only the myths of segmental purity, of compartmentalized responsibility, could sustain the argument that by concentrating on matters at home Americans were, after all, putting first things first, probably doing all they could. Although domestic and international abuses grew from the same broad social sources, they not only exacted horribly different human costs but also lent themselves to very different correctives. The deficiencies of a public, developing from the deepest national traditions, were subject to at least certain restraints inherent in a segmented society: a neighborhood suffocating in garbage would eventually insist upon its removal, a newly assertive group would demand greater access to the nation's medical resources, a band of cheated consumers would press for modifications in business autonomy. By the rules of the American game, these incessant encounters set some outer limits to the excesses of the modern system at home.

Wholesale exports of oppression, on the other hand, dated from the 1940s, a compression of events scarcely deserving the title of tradition. Except in the case of the Middle East, no strong network of domestic interests demanded these decisions. Nor in most instances could weaker nations protect themselves from American intrusions. It had fallen largely within the discretion of a small, detached government circle to ignore Greek insurgency, oust Jacobo Arbenz from Guatemala, abandon Patrice Lumumba in the Congo, and embargo Fidel Castro in Cuba; to reinforce Francisco Franco in Spain, Syngman Rhee in South Korea, and the military chieftains in Latin America; to control the flow of international credits into impoverished lands, export bombs instead of bread, and determine how much nutrition would alleviate how much starvation in South Asia or Africa. Neither global necessities nor national imperatives dictated these decisions. The great lesson of the 1960s—that the cratered villages of Vietnam marked a purely arbitrary American line of defense—applied equally to an array of less dramatized interventions and constraints since the 1940s. A handful of executive officials had made their own calculations of the appropriate human price for international order, and here, unlike any basic area of domestic life, a new President could make a profound difference. The consequences of American power need not cry terror in the night, if someone would only listen.

# Notes

### I On Waking from an American Dream

p. 6 J. Hector St. John Crèvecœur: *Letters from an American Farmer* (Fox, Duffield edition, 1904), p. 49.

### II The Units of Life

p. 35 Michael Zuckerman: *Peaceable Kingdoms* (1970), p. 225.
p. 37 James Bryce: *The American Commonwealth,* 2 vols. (2nd revised edition, 1891), II, 315.
p. 37 Alexis de Tocqueville: *Democracy in America,* 2 vols., ed. Phillips Bradley (Vintage edition, 1954), I, 299-300.

### III Liberty, Equality, and Segregation

p. 49 Hans L. Trefousse: *The Radical Republicans* (1969), p. 56.
p. 53 Jonathan Turner quoted in Don Harrison Doyle, "Chaos and Community in a Frontier Town" (Ph.D. Dissertation, 1973), p. 238.
p. 53 M. A. De Wolfe Howe: *John Jay Chapman and His Letters* (1937), p. 218.
p. 58 *America of the Fifties: Letters of Fredrika Bremer,* ed. Adolph B. Benson (1924), p. 72.

p. 62 *Chicago Sun-Times* (March 25, 1972), p. 2.

p. 68 David Brion Davis, "Some Themes of Counter-Subversion: An Analysis of Anti-Masonic, Anti-Catholic, and Anti-Mormon Literature," *Mississippi Valley Historical Review*, XLVII (Sept. 1960), 212.

p. 70 Michael E. Parrish: *Securities Regulation and the New Deal* (1970), p. 130.

p. 74 Roger M. Sherman quoted in Early Lee Fox: *The American Colonization Society, 1817-1840* (1919), p. 36.

p. 75 Sherwood Anderson, "Maury Maverick in San Antonio," *New Republic*, CII (March 25, 1940), 398.

p. 84 Edward Beecher: *Narrative of Riots at Alton* (E. P. Dutton edition, 1965), pp. 58-59.

p. 89 Larzer Ziff: *The American 1890s* (1966), p. 288.

## IV  A Whole Society

p. 90 *The Portable Hawthorne*, ed. Malcolm Cowley (revised edition, 1969), p. 687.

p. 93 "Number Two," *The Federalist (Modern Library edition*, n. d.), p. 9.

p. 115 Horace Mann quoted in John L. Thomas, "Romantic Reform in America, 1815-1865," *American Quarterly*, XVII (Winter 1965), 669.

p. 115 David Rothman: *The Discovery of the Asylum* (1971), p. 174.

## V  The Politics of the Social Contract

p. 126 Bernard R. Crick: *In Defense of Politics* (1962), p. 28.

p. 130 James Bryce: *The American Commonwealth*, 2 vols. (2nd revised edition, 1891), II, 349-350.

p. 152 David Grimsted, "Rioting in Its Jacksonian Setting," *American Historical Review*, LXXVII (April 1972), 367.

p. 161 Samuel P. Huntington: *The Common Defense* (1961), p. 193.

p. 164 Hannah Arendt, "Reflections on Power," *New York Review of Books* (Feb. 27, 1969), p. 24.

p. 164  *The Two Trials of John Fries on an Indictment for Treason* (1800), p. 29.

### VI Consequences

p. 170  Robert K. Merton: *Social Theory and Social Structure* (1949), p. 134.

p. 170  Henry James: *The American Scene* (1907), pp. 120, 118.

p. 176  J. Joseph Huthmacher: *Senator Robert F. Wagner and the Rise of Urban Liberalism* (1968), p. 265.

p. 177  Rocco C. Siciliano quoted in *New York Times* (June 29, 1970), p. 1.

p. 186  Ernst Topitsch, "World Interpretation and Self-Interpretation: Some Basic Patterns," in *Myth and Mythmaking*, ed. Henry A. Murray (1960), p. 157.

p. 192  Adlai E. Stevenson: *Call to Greatness* (1954), pp. 5-7.